Advance Praise

Justin delivers an honest and poignant account of his personal journey at Penn State and beyond. A must-read for all who will appreciate an in-depth look into life as a student-athlete under legendary coach Joe Paterno.

– Kerry Collins, PSU '94, retired NFL quarterback

I played for Penn State many years before Justin, but one unique thing about Penn State is that we both played under the same head coach and many of the same assistant coaches. Justin's love and loyalty to Penn State, Penn State football, and Joe Paterno mimic the feelings (and experiences) for me and so many other Penn State football lettermen. Justin captures and relates those feelings in a real way that lettermen AND the general public can relate to and enjoy. Job well done!

– Dr. Ray (Buddy) Tesner '75, cofounder of the PSU Football Letterman's Club

More Than the Jersey is exactly what its title promises: a story that transcends sport and goes straight to the heart of what it means to struggle, grow, and become. Dr. Justin Williams tells his life with remarkable openness, moving from serious to funny to tender with the ease of someone who has made peace with every chapter. This is a book that will move you, make you laugh, and leave you thinking long after you've finished—bring it home and pass it around.

—Dana Dokmanovich Harris, PSU '72, board member of The Pittsburgh Promise

Justin captures the grit, brotherhood, and soul of Penn State football like no one else. *More Than the Jersey* is a heartfelt story about finding yourself while honoring the game we love. Reading Justin's journey reminded me of what it means to be part of something bigger than yourself. This memoir is a must-read for anyone who loves football, identity, and the lessons in between.

—Kyle Brady, Esquire, '94, Penn State football letterman, retired NFL tight end

Dr. Williams's book captures the essence of Joe Paterno's "Grand Experiment"—the belief that a university can achieve both academic excellence and athletic success without sacrificing either. Through a powerful firsthand account, he reflects on the lasting impact of that philosophy and the enduring legacy carried forward by those shaped by it.

—Anthony Gordon '78, PSU football letterman

Justin Williams's vulnerability offers a rare and honest look at what it takes to confront self-doubt, perform under pressure, and ultimately discover who you are. Two decades earlier, I walked a similar path—learning those same hard lessons under the same legendary coach, Joe Paterno. *More Than the Jersey* is more than a football story—it's about becoming who you're meant to be. If you're chasing a dream, read it, and you'll understand what we truly mean when we say: We Are... Penn State.

– Steve Davis, '73, Penn State football letterman, and CEO/founder of Human Relations Institute

Justin Williams: father, husband, friend, author, teacher, and a change maker. His passion for scholarship and equity was quickly apparent upon our first meeting, something that quickly stood out among his peers. He is truly a leader and passionate about youth success, as he knows firsthand what opportunity can lead to.

– Curt Marshall, PSU '86, retired director of Diversity Recruitment and Retention at Penn State's College of Arts and Architecture

In Dr. Justin S. Williams's new book, *More Than the Jersey*, college football fans will get a descriptive view of what life was like for a college football recruit and eventual player at Penn State University during head coach Joe Paterno's most notable years of victorious accomplishments in the early 1990s. But Dr. William's book represents more than just that.

The author offers a highly detailed look at the decisions he made while in college and playing for Coach Paterno, a man he came to greatly admire. He also presents a solemn look at Paterno's life and legacy that many people outside the Penn State University sphere could never have known before.

Finally, Dr. Williams also delves deeply into his own life, and in the many profound chapters of this book, he presents to us stories of the vital relationships that he experienced throughout his years at Penn State, both on campus and on the football field. It is those relationships that helped make him the man he is today, and that form the strength of this book.

More Than the Jersey is a book that will give readers a wakeup call into an individual's experiences during perhaps the most important years of his life... his college years at one of America's greatest institutions, Penn State University. I highly recommend it.

—Joe Zagorski, Pro Football Writers of America, and author of *From the Outhouse to the Penthouse*

More Than the Jersey

More Than the Jersey

Playing for Joe at the Intersection of Football and Identity

Dr. Justin S. Williams

HIGHLANDER PRESS

This is a work of nonfiction. It is a memoir based on the author's experiences and memory. Some names, identifying details, and minor characteristics have been changed to protect individuals' privacy. Any such changes are not intended to alter the substance of events. Certain dialogue has been reconstructed to reflect the essence of conversations and the author's best recollection.

ISBN: 978-1-956442-69-4
ebook ISBN: 978-1-956442-70-0
Library of Congress Control Number: Applied for

Published by Highlander Press
501 W. University Pkwy, Suite B-2
Baltimore, MD 21210

Cover design: Alexander van Ness (www.nessgraphica.com)
Editor: Deborah Kevin, MA (www.deborahkevin.com)

For Nittany Nation, my Penn State football brothers; my four children, Hannah, Ty, Nnamdi, and Aria; my parents, Gloria and Dennis Williams; and the man to whom they gladly sent me to finish what they started, Joseph Vincent Paterno.

Finally, I dedicate this book to Sue Paterno and her family. The price paid by the wife and children of a legend is always significant. Without their sacrifice, this book would not be possible.

We're all products of the people we meet in our life.

— Joseph V. Paterno

Contents

Foreword

Suzanne Pohland Paterno, American philanthropist, PSU '62

More Than the Jersey tells about the journey Justin Williams took from his birth in Dulwich, England, to Uniondale, to Penn State in State College. The settings differ among athletes, but what they feel, how they grow and mature, the triumphs, the setbacks, and the physical pain they endure are part of each athlete's journey to maturity. Justin documents all these emotions honestly.

Justin also gives credit to those who helped him on his journey. His dad's example of how a great athlete behaves, trains, and competes influenced him as he grew. Different coaches played distinct roles in his life and helped him succeed through competition. The best ones also guided him in finding the right path in his life. He analyzed how their interactions helped him learn who he was as he struggled to become a man. It was not always easy or natural, plus he had to deal with the race issue. Could he let it affect his life and his relationships with others? Or did he embrace his being and use what he learned to educate others?

Through Justin's self-examination, he found his passion, his role, and his future. He teaches others to strive for excellence and successfully leads them to find themselves. Justin's journey has miles to go, but his evaluation of those around him and of himself will drive him to perfection.

Prologue

WHY IN THE WORLD SHOULD YOU READ THIS BOOK? MY NAME alone isn't reason enough. In our celebrity-conscious, material world, I do not have the recognition of various other Nittany Lions who will be my teammates and friends for all time, hallowed names in Penn State lore like Kerry Collins (K. C.), Ki-Jana Carter (Kee), Bobby Engram (Bubba), O. J. McDuffie (Juice), Jon Witman (Wit), or Jeff Hartings (Hartman). I did not accomplish anywhere near what these men did on our home turf at Beaver Stadium, nor in various stadiums across the country. I'll not be remembered for anything I did on the field.

So, what qualifies me to write a book about my Penn State football experience? First, I have the energy and desire to do so. If it were easy to do, many others would have already done so. After all, Penn State football players know how to write. A whole roster of us—right in line with Penn State football's 93 percent graduation rate—walked away with diplomas in hand, which isn't something many of our brothers across the country can say after being pushed to give everything on the field for institutions that didn't always give back. But despite our intellectual acumen, writing first-person accounts of our time playing for a legendary coach and program hasn't been a top priority.

In fact, I know of only one book like this that has so far been written by former players: a father-and-son tandem, Charles and Tony Pittman. Considering Tony and I were teammates for four years, I think it'll be interesting to see the differences and similarities in what we found important or intriguing. It may also be interesting to readers, given the differing backgrounds in each case: He has a father who also played for the same coach, and I am an immigrant whose earliest memory of Penn State football was the national championship victory over the University of Miami in January 1987. Around 1,500 men can claim they played football at Penn State for Joe Paterno, and only *three* of them (two books, counting this one) so far have published a book documenting what it was like. That's somewhat peculiar, wouldn't you say?

Secondly, many of my brothers who would probably write equally, if not more entertaining, memoirs than mine don't have the time. You see, they majored in things like engineering, medicine, business administration, accounting, and economics, or they've been extremely busy with their lives as professional athletes and the celebrity and business opportunities that arise as a result. I, on the other hand, have more time to concern myself with writing and getting my story out there in a way only a Penn State football letterman can. I majored in English education and have taught English in New York and abroad for more than a quarter of a century.

Finally, my individual Penn State football story is more representative of most young men who played for Joe Paterno in State College, Pennsylvania. Only a handful of them were "hot shots," as Joe would say. My story is the story of a guy blessed with enough physical talent to have gone to many schools throughout our country via a football, track, or baseball scholarship, but who chose to be a part of The Pennsylvania State University and its football program with a legendary head coach. I had great athletic and academic potential, but neither side of who I was then panned out exactly the way I envisioned. I had my time to shine but never got to be "The Guy" on campus.

This is my story, one that men who played at the highest level of college football can recognize and relate to, whether they were superstars or scout team All-Americans. Mine is the story of the guy somewhere in the middle, more closely aligned with the stars than the scout teamers, though I do not put myself above nor beneath any man with whom I played. I was the guy with enough talent and polish to be a star at his university, but who came up short.

"Came up short" is a phrase that might rub some the wrong way. I understand that millions of schoolboys would have done anything to put on our beautifully plain uniforms and ride the bench for four or five years; anything to come out of that tunnel on game day to a sea of Nittany Lion faithful. I wasn't bred to be satisfied with just making it to Penn State, however. Although I became a backup as my time progressed, I was always viewed as one of the leaders of my class, then eventually one of the more outspoken leaders of the team. Some guys with a similar big-time college football legacy blame others for why their light didn't shine as bright as the very brightest. I used to have some of these feelings also, but I grew up.

In sharing my memories and analysis (good, bad, and ugly) of my time as a student-athlete at the gorgeous University Park campus, you'll learn about what it's like to play for a legend. Not just any legend, however, but one who, irrespective of your take on him, stands in a class totally alone. If you are looking for a memoir written by a disgruntled former player who wishes to show the world how Coach Paterno's "Grand Experiment" didn't work for him, this is not the book for you.

Pregame

Spring 1991

It's a gorgeous journey from Long Island, New York, to State College, Pennsylvania. Once you get past the eternally congested Cross Bronx Expressway and across the George Washington Bridge into New Jersey, otherwise known as the first hour of the trip, you have about three hours remaining to listen to the news, a podcast on satellite radio, or some quality music on one of your playlists. The scenery is usually green, mountainous, while you steadily ascend and then descend into the valley famous for being happy.

I've made the trip many times and in various ways, at least a hundred times, as I write this sentence in September 2025, exactly four days before I retake the trip to witness the spectacle and pageantry of our nationally renowned White Out game. My first time alone at University Park, the main campus of The Pennsylvania State University, was special for all the reasons a first time would be.

I remember the anticipatory and anxious feeling I had as the bus decelerated for the Penn State exit off Interstate 80. From there, it was about another twenty miles before I could see the campus, but it felt longer because I thought every mile would be the last. As I looked to my left from my window seat, rural towns that exemplified much of America scrolled by. This was well before the highway bypass was completed, which now makes these last few miles move past more quickly and uneventfully, a good or bad thing, depending.

I noticed the blue-and-white colored Penn State Sub Shop, unexpectedly far from downtown State College; the lack of sidewalks, with front doors of homes surprisingly close to the road; the single lane road we were on that had enough traffic before us to make this final leg of the trip exasperating; the state penitentiary (state pen), whose ironic location and title, just up the road, was immediately apparent to me; crossing over the train tracks then passing the Nittany Mall on the right; making an easy left as the Long John Silver's restaurant went by on the right, followed by what was soon to be one of my favorite places to eat in State College, Damon's Grill, about half a mile further and also on the right; then making a right onto campus, seeing Beaver Stadium, in all its Lego-like constructed, starship magnificence, as if on a launchpad about to shoot its inhabitants off into the stars. It seated only 93,000 then.

As we pulled up in front of Holuba Hall, the indoor football facility with two fifty-yard practice fields harboring turf that shaved off the top layer of skin even if you tripped and fell on it, my stomach butterflies were in full churn. But I was neither intimidated nor frightened. The five hours on that first bus ride felt familiar.

Origins

I WAS BORN AT DULWICH HOSPITAL, IN A SMALL TOWN OF THE same name, a southern suburb of London, England, in February of 1973. Most of the hospital no longer exists, replaced by updated community health facilities. The original hospital was built in the late 1800s. With its red-brick exterior, large windows that let in plenty of air and sunlight, and other architectural features, it would not look like a hospital to many Americans in the 1970s.

King's College Hospital, Dulwich, England, where I was born.

England, like the rest of Europe, embodied a unique mixture of the old and new world. As a boy in England, however, it was, to me, the entire world. England was also very overcast, rainy, and therefore extremely green. Every town seemed to have a community park with gorgeously kept mazes carved out of hedges. Additionally, red was a ubiquitous color. Besides red bricks, red vertical mailboxes, red telephone booths, and red double-decker buses were everywhere. I wasn't aware I was in the "old world" until I arrived in the new.

My parents had emigrated to London separately from the Caribbean islands of Jamaica and Trinidad. My mother completed high school in Trinidad in 1959. Soon after, she made her way to England to study nursing. Dad made his way to South London with my grandparents in 1963. He was thirteen years old. Sometime around 1970, they met in South London. Mom was twenty-seven, and Dad was twenty. They married a year and a month before I was born.

Saint Faiths Center, where my parents were married and where I was baptized in England.

My father, Dennis Anthony Williams, born in Ocho Rios, Jamaica, was a fast bowler (similar to a power pitcher in baseball) on one of the best cricket teams ever to be assembled at the Dulwich Cricket Club, which dates back to 1867. To this day, their team photo is a significant part of club history. I have the very same photo featured prominently in my home.

I have warm, palpable memories of being a child and being part of my father's cricket matches. The largely rural grounds, with manicured cricket and croquet playing areas, mimicked amateur facilities of the time. There was no arena seating for onlookers. You either sat in your car and watched, as mom did to keep an eye on my sister and I, watched from the clubhouse, brought a picnic blanket or the relatively new (at the time) lawn chairs to sit and watch. I remember comments of admiration from opposing players uttered to my mother, feeling the inquisitive eyes of enthusiasts in and around the oval (ballpark), and being in the buzzing, chipper clubhouse with my father after games. I have photos from the 1970s, taken by journalists, of my father, stills that capture how impressive an athlete he was. My pride in and respect for him, and in turn, my name, were an overwhelming ingredient in the burgeoning essence of who I was as a kid and what I have become as a man. Like so many of my Penn State teammates, as well as great athletes of any ilk, athleticism runs in the family.

England, as well as Europe, is a series of interconnected small, quaint towns and villages with intermittent splashes of cosmopolitan, historic, big cities. As a young British West Indian lad, I remember taking a long drive with my parents to a vacation in the southwestern town of Cornwall, an area famous for its beaches, beach communities, and vacation residences. I remember us staying in a trailer for vacationers. There was a large public swimming pool, and I remember playing in it and befriending a light-complexioned boy. It was the summer of 1979, just over a year before Mom and Dad decided to make the leap to America.

My sister and I sitting in our living room in Sidcup, England, in the mid-1970s. Photo credit: Dennis Williams.

The British aspect of my childhood left indelible impressions. I remember strawberry picking, pony rides, and trips to study London's shipbuilding history. It is impossible for me to forget the rigid academic environment of Saint Joseph's Convent, a private school for boys run by nuns, where I attended until I was almost eight years old. The uniform, complete with a tie I learned to tie myself by the age of five; standing up in class each time I either volunteered or was called upon to provide an answer or ask a question; the ruler across the back of my hands or meter stick on the leg for various infractions committed, all were harbingers of an educational environment my graduate program at Penn State, years later, would refer to as "high academic press." I was accepted into this school because my dad was a star on the Dulwich team. He was the only melanated player. The team's owner also made sure my mom and dad had a nice home to move into soon after they got married on January 1, 1972.

They moved from a top-floor apartment in a house on a street called Half Moon Lane in Dulwich to a very comfortable two-floor home on a property shaped like an elongated rectangle on East Rochester Way in Sidcup, Kent, also in South London. Beginning after World War II, Afro-Caribbean people living in island nations colonized by England began streaming into South London, settling in and around Brixton (a rough equivalent to Harlem, New York, in the 1920s) to take advantage of the many job opportunities within the working-class sector. My paternal grandmother was a seamstress. Her husband was a gambler and philanderer. My parents managed to do a bit better for themselves. Mom was a registered nurse, and Dad worked for British Telecommunications. Dad got a vasectomy after my sister was born in 1976. He didn't want to be like his father, who made children all over Jamaica that he didn't support.

My childhood home in Sidcup, England. Photo credit: Dennis Williams.

Mingling with part of the British elite as a school child, Buckingham Palace, Parliament, Big Ben, and Piccadilly Circus were everyday experiences for me as a very aware seven-year-old, just as the Empire State Building, the Statue of Liberty, suburban Long Island, and the Twin Towers would become close and personal for me by the time I was eleven. My upbringing wired me to see central Pennsylvania as a natural extension of who I was.

The suburban town of Uniondale, New York, felt less dense, population-wise, quieter, and much more diverse than my neighborhood in Sidcup, South London. Outside of my British home was a highway. Although my English garden was larger, my American backyard had an in-ground swimming pool.

My parents didn't need to leave England, but Dad was curious, and Mom was willing to go along for the ride. They applied for their visas, expecting to hear back in maybe a year. Three months later, they learned that "the land of opportunity" was ready to take them on. So, they went, knowing that if things didn't work out, they wouldn't be stuck.

My sister Natasha and I posing outside our childhood home on the day of my sixth-grade graduation. Photo credit: Dennis Williams.

Everything I knew was in the United Kingdom. I cried many tears from my last day at convent school until our arrival at John F. Kennedy Airport a few weeks later in Queens County, one of the two boroughs of New York City, on the landmass known as Long Island. Uniondale was only a fifteen-minute easterly drive. Penn State and Joe Paterno were still eleven years away.

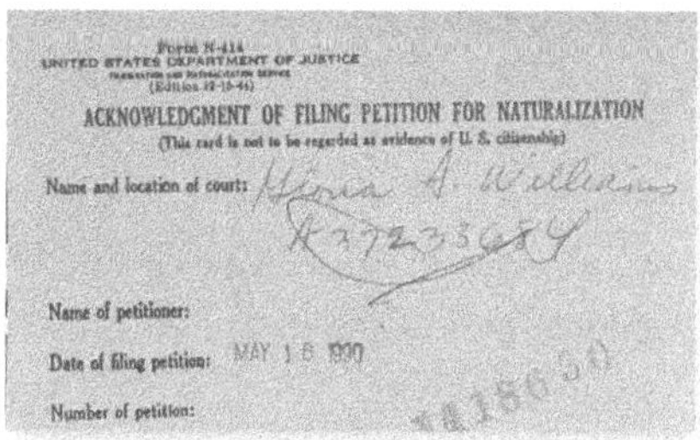

Form N-414
UNITED STATES DEPARTMENT OF JUSTICE
(Edition 12-15-46)
ACKNOWLEDGMENT OF FILING PETITION FOR NATURALIZATION
(This card is not to be regarded as evidence of U. S. citizenship)
Name and location of court:
Name of petitioner:
Date of filing petition:
Number of petition:

My mother's naturalization petition.

Form N-414
UNITED STATES DEPARTMENT OF JUSTICE
(Edition 12-15-46)
ACKNOWLEDGMENT OF FILING PETITION FOR NATURALIZATION
(This card is not to be regarded as evidence of U. S. citizenship)
Name and location of court:
Name of petitioner:
Date of filing petition:
Number of petition:

My father's naturalization petition.

Being Recruited

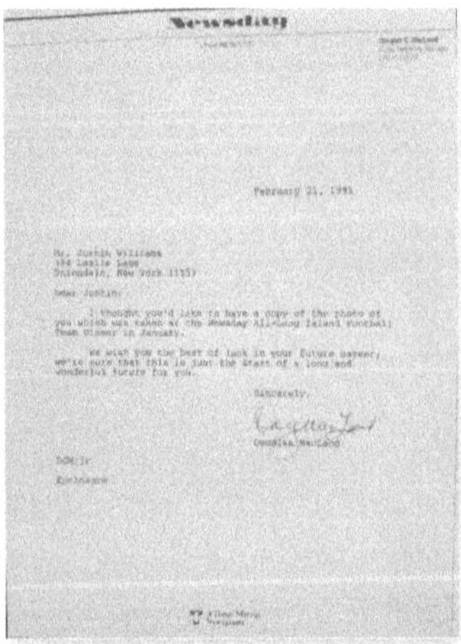

Newsday

February 21, 199[illegible]

Mr. Justin Williams
194 Leslie Lane
Uniondale, New York 11553

Dear Justin:

I thought you'd like to have a copy of the photo of you which was taken at the Newsday All-Long Island Football Team Dinner in January.

We wish you the best of luck in your future career; we're sure that this is just the start of a long and wonderful future for you.

Sincerely,

Douglas [illegible]

[illegible]

Enclosure

A letter from Newsday sent to me.

As it turned out, Penn State linebackers coach Joe "Buddy" Sarra's no frills, direct, honest recruiting approach appealed to my upbringing. I didn't need to be fawned over. I didn't need to be told how good I was. I didn't need to be bribed with girls, money, or other things.

Many other programs recruiting me were doing all that. My entire life, I was provided what I needed and enough of what I wanted. This made me better off than some of my PSU teammates, but all of us were attracted to the blue-collar demeanor and demands of the Penn State football program.

My dad drove me in his burgundy 1988 Nissan Pathfinder to the spot just off the Long Island Expressway where we met the bus that would take me to Penn State University's main campus, University

Park, where I would spend the next four days away from my parents for the first time in my life. Besides us figuring out where the bus would be, we didn't talk much about this being my first time away from him without being with family. This meant Dad knew I was ready. As I got out of the SUV to get on the bus, he told me to have fun, something he always told me. It's one of the most important things he always said to me, besides "I love you" or "I'm proud of you." Too many parents put too much pressure on their children to succeed.

The Male Athlete of the Year plaque I won in my last year of junior high school.

I was headed to a four-day, four-practice-per-day football camp for high school-age young men. The bus was filled with players from Walt Witman High School in Suffolk County, New York. Coach Sarra coordinated with Rich Cariddi, Witman's head coach at the time, to help me attend the camp more easily.

I was the only person on the bus from my school, Uniondale High School, located in Nassau County, the same town where the New York Islanders used to play at the Nassau Coliseum. No more than a quarter of a mile from the coliseum, I watched the New York Jets practice at Hofstra University until the National Football League (NFL) franchise moved to its current location in Florham Park, New Jersey, in 2008. At that time in my life,

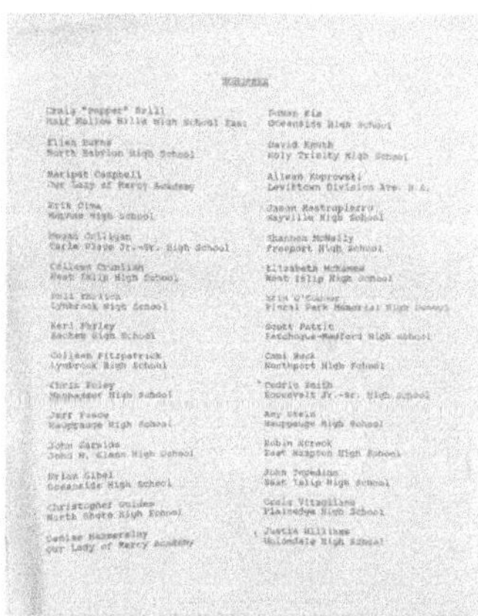

News 12 Scholar Athlete Award Reception honorees.

playing for the Jets wasn't yet something I thought possible. The bus I caught took me to the place where I realized being a professional football player was actually possible.

I was a rising high school senior. It was late June 1990. There were two future Penn State football players on that bus that day, and I was one. The other was a rising high school junior. Years later, I attended his bachelor party in Montreal, Canada. Even more years later, I attended his fiftieth birthday celebration. We both remain Long Islanders and brothers to this day. His name is Gerald Filardi.

My Gridiron 1990 Conference plaque.

I will always be extremely grateful to Joe Sarra for handling himself the way he did during Penn State's recruitment of me. Within the class of '91, he recruited three blue chippers from Long Island. The other two were Andre—or Dre—Johnson, and Marco Rivera. Andre was a fully grown man the first time I saw him. He is your prototypical six-foot-seven-inch quiet type with a big laugh, kind, warm disposition, and huge hands that render you immobile once they are upon you. I discovered that attribute later during the few times I was foolish enough to even pretend to play-fight with him at Nittany Apartments on campus, where we lived as roommates. Dre attended Southampton High School in the southern part of Suffolk County, Long Island, at least an hour-and-a-half's drive east of my hometown. Like so many guys I played with at Penn State and those I

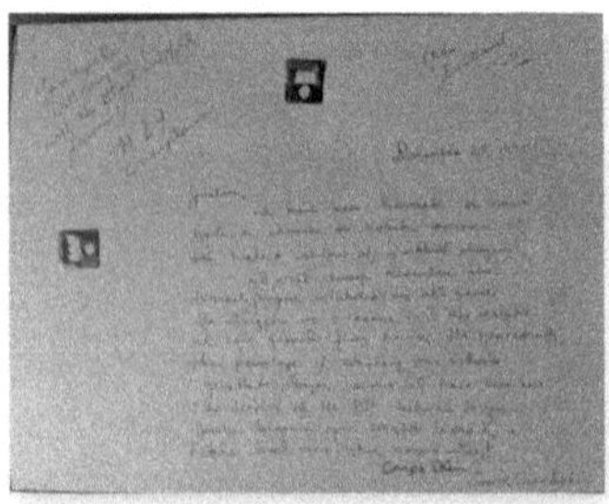

Letter from my high school head football coach, written on the back of a photo frame.

played against across the nation, he was a man among boys as a high school athlete.

Marco starred at Elmont High School in Nassau County, right on the border with the New York City borough of Queens, about a twenty-minute drive west from my hometown. I first met him as a member of Nassau County's high school football all-star team in December 1990. He wasn't as tall as Dre, but his feet were just as quick, quicker probably. By '93, Marco and Andre were stalwarts on a Penn State offensive line that would eventually become one of the greatest in Penn State football history. Marco would go on to win a Super Bowl title as a key member of Brett Favre's offensive line with the Green Bay Packers. The common denominator for Marco, Dre, and me was Joe "Buddy" Sarra.

Buddy's recruiting style was no-nonsense. He didn't talk to me like other recruiters had. He wasn't interested in winning me over by telling me what he thought I wanted to hear. He didn't try to appeal to my ego or my sense of vanity. He talked to me like I was a young person who had a good head on his shoulders, capable of handling some straight talk. That was my introduction to what we refer to as "Penn State Proud."

Buddy never talked to me about coeds who wanted to meet me, nor did he offer me the world. During our conversations leading up to my first visit, it was clear that Penn State was interested in me, but I didn't get the sense that Buddy was drooling on himself on the other end of the phone. Other recruiters had certainly given me that sense, making me feel they'd say or do just about anything to get me to come take an official visit to their campuses.

My recruiting process began in earnest in the spring of 1990. And even though it was "only" a few months in, it felt like two years—because when your kitchen phone rings every night, time does that stretchy thing. I was researching schools, comparing promises, listening to pitches, and calling adults I trusted to sanity-check what I was hearing. The whole thing was flattering, overwhelming, and weirdly heavy for an eighteen-year-old—*and this was the early nineties*, before the sleepless internet, recruiting sites, and social media hot takes. Today's version of that process? With money flying around and everybody with an opinion and a platform? Yikes. It was easy to get lost back then. Now? I don't even want to imagine.

And some of it was... off.

One university even had women calling my home, claiming to be students (I assume they were, but you never know), assuring me I'd "have a good time" if I visited. Another assistant coach at an eastern school spent half his energy comparing his university, his program, and his stadium to Penn State's—as if repeating "we're just like them" enough times would make it true. He knew Penn State was the "Beast of the East," and he knew he was battling the Nittany Lions for my talents.

Then, on one of our last calls, he said the quiet part out loud. He told me I should attend his school because "there's more of your kind here" than at Penn State.

I didn't argue. I didn't debate. I handed the phone to my dad. I was completely turned off.

And yes—lines like that probably worked on plenty of young men. That doesn't make them foolish or me some genius. But it *does* say something about how different homes raise people. That mentality wasn't the cup of tea I was raised to drink.

That's part of what made Penn State feel so different. Joe "Buddy" Sarra and Joe Paterno weren't selling me a vibe. They were selling me something rare in recruiting: consistency.

Buddy did things by the book—literally. He once slept in his rental car in front of my house because it would have been an NCAA violation to see me off campus the night before the first legal day coaches could visit recruits at home. That's how strict—and how deliberate—he was.

I saw that same "do it right" approach on campus. During a high school football camp visit to Penn State that June, Coach Sarra made me run behind his car so I could meet Coach Paterno—because driving me a quarter-mile would have been an NCAA violation. It sounds ridiculous now. It probably *was* ridiculous. But it also told me something: these guys weren't improvising their integrity.

By that point, in today's terms, I would've been considered a five-star player. After my senior season, I was rated an All-American by *Super Prep* magazine. And the year before that—my junior season—I quarterbacked the highest scoring offense on Long Island, out of about one hundred high schools. Schools knew who I was. And they called accordingly.

The unofficial visit that changed everything took place over the weekend of August 2, 1990. My parents and I went to State College, and Penn State made an impression that was hard to ignore. Buddy, Joe—everybody we met left us feeling like this place cared about the person *and* the player.

A 1990 Gridiron Banquet ticket.

But one person, in particular, sealed it for my parents: Jim Caldwell.

Coach Caldwell drove us around State College that weekend. My parents loved him immediately. And they didn't dance around it, either. They asked him straight up whether they could trust him to watch out for me if I went to Penn State. He made them feel at ease in a way that mattered. It wasn't a sales pitch. It wasn't a recruiting line. It was steadiness.

My parents loved the visit overall.

And what struck me most was how careful they were on the drive back to Long Island. They were clearly impressed, but they didn't want to come across as pushy. Still, they said something that stuck: State College reminded them of England. It felt familiar to them in a way they didn't expect. And they told me, gently, that they wouldn't mind at all if I ended up there.

What they wanted—what any parents worth their salt wanted—was to know I'd be in the hands of good people who cared about more than football. By the time we got home, they were believers.

After that visit, I called Coach Caldwell and asked if he would be there for my entire stay. I was enamored with him, but I wasn't naive about coaching. Even at eighteen, I understood the turnstile nature of college and pro football jobs.

He said what he could honestly say at the time: he had no plans to leave, and he expected to be there throughout my time.

He accepted the head coaching job at Wake Forest after my sophomore year.

I wasn't mad at him at all. Back then, brown-complexioned men at the helm of big-time college programs were few and far between. And if we were being honest, things still hadn't improved nearly enough. I was proud to have been in his orbit at all—proud that he rose to the pinnacle of the profession, including a Super Bowl appearance as a head coach. I was proud I got to be in his circle, if only for a minute.

Like so many others, Coach Caldwell and I were bound forever by Penn State and Joe Paterno. And in a funny way, Penn State had already started binding me to people during that first summer—before I ever signed anything.

That same camp introduced me to another standout—this kid from Pennsylvania, about six foot two, who could move better than any athlete that size I had ever seen. We sized each other up all week, measuring ourselves the way athletes always did. We didn't have to say a word about it. The competition happened anyway, plain as day. Even years later, the feeling from that week stayed palpable to me.

Here was the part I couldn't have known then: He and I ended up sitting next to each other in the Penn State football locker room for five years, simply because our last names fell one after the other in the alphabet. We made each other laugh constantly during some of the most formative years of our lives. And later, he became a Super Bowl champion with the Pittsburgh Steelers.

His name was Jon Witman.

The day after we returned from State College, Buddy called. I must've sounded pretty impressed—he was probably used to that tone once a family saw what Penn State had to offer. That's when he raised the idea of a verbal commitment and explained what it meant: Penn State would guarantee my spot at University Park and honor the scholarship no matter what happened during my senior year—even if I got badly hurt.

"Guaranteed. No matter what."

He told me to think about it.

I did. I talked to my parents. I talked to a few other people I trusted. And on August 9, 1990—about a month before senior year started and a couple of weeks before my final high school season began—I verbally committed to Penn State.

Me with Joe "Buddy" Sarra.

To me, it felt like a no-brainer.

For one thing, Joe Paterno wrote me four handwritten letters that summer, starting the week I returned from camp in June. Believe it or not, I didn't fully grasp what that meant. A man in his position doesn't do that unless he wants you. In one letter he wrote, "I've never coached a player from England before." That not-so-subtle hint somehow still went right over my head and beneath my shoes. I was so stunned by the surrealness of Joe Paterno writing *me* that I didn't even want to believe I was being offered a scholarship.

But after our visit, Buddy made Joe's subtext plain: They wanted me. Period.

And my reaction, honestly, was: Who the hell am I at eighteen to say, "Thanks, Coach, but I think I'll weigh my options"? What options were better than this?

Where else could I be far enough from home to become my own

person, but close enough that family and friends could visit? What other school within 500 miles offered big-time football, a first-class education, and a true large-campus experience? Who had a bigger stadium? Who was talking about mandatory study hall four days a week for freshmen? And who else had a living legend running a program that graduated his players—especially those with darker skin—at a higher rate than almost anybody competing at that level?

For me, only one university checked every box.

I was also relieved to be done. I was tired of the phone calls. The kitchen phone never stopped ringing. I got over one hundred letters from colleges across the country—three high-topped sneaker boxes worth. I kept stacks of business cards from head coaches who were interested. I didn't want to string anybody along. I wasn't interested in wasting anyone's time.

I planned to take one official visit and one official visit only: Penn State. But there was one school that just would not let go.

Indiana, along with Syracuse, Rutgers, and Wisconsin, came after me hard once the college season ended in January 1990. Most of those calls stopped after my father and I told them I was committed to Penn State. Indiana didn't.

I don't remember the recruiter's name, but I remember his persistence. He was relentless, and he was convincing enough that I told him I'd visit.

To his credit, he immediately said, "You ought to inform Penn State that you're planning to take a visit here."

My eighteen-year-old brain tried to do the math and come up with a loophole. I figured I could take the trip without telling Buddy—assuming Penn State would never find out. The Indiana coach knew better, and I respect him for being straight with me. He didn't have to be.

So, I brought it to Buddy.

He was calm, but firm. He explained that a verbal commitment meant my recruiting process was over—and that visiting another university would be a step backward from our agreement. Penn

State's side of the deal was clear: The scholarship was guaranteed no matter what happened during my senior year. My side of the deal needed to mean something, too.

I already knew what he was going to say before he said it. I just didn't know how to tell Indiana, plainly, that I didn't want to come. But I'm glad I didn't go on any other official visits. I probably would've gotten pulled into confusion—because I know now how schools roll out the red carpet for recruits. Ending the process early gave me clarity. And I have no regrets about it.

The Penn State class coming in behind me was loaded. Three kids from Long Island—Marco, Andre, and me—were part of what many believed was the best recruiting class in America coming out of high school in 1991. Penn State faithful will immediately recognize names like Bobby Engram, Ki-Jana Carter, Michael Archie, Stephen Pitts, Jeff Hartings, Keith Conlin, Jon Witman, Willie Smith, and Brian Milne—great football players and fine men.

And there are other names from that class I'll never forget: Cliff Dingle, Brian King, Wayne Holmes, Lionel Fayard Jr., Dave Thomas, Justin Wheeler, Brad Johnson, Scott Stratton, J. T. Morris, and Ricky Roe.

My senior year I ran up my parents' phone bill—listening to recruiting hotlines for updates about who was thinking about committing and who had already committed. (They were pissed. This was a few years before the World Wide Web. There was no "just look it up.")

Not all of us finished our careers at Penn State. Not all of us had the careers we wanted there—me included. But my story, in its own way, helps explain the larger story: the reality of what it means for young men to pass through a program and a university that, together, forge a particular kind of Penn State experience.

Fast-forward to the end of it: I graduated from Uniondale High School on Sunday, June 23, 1991. The ceremony was held on the front lawn in the afternoon.

And if I'm being honest, the second semester of my senior year was spent more in my bedroom than in class—not because I didn't care, but because my life had shifted into this strange in-between season. Ten months earlier, Buddy had explained the guarantee: If I committed, my ticket to University Park was secure, no matter what.

He was right. I was on the University Park campus with my parents by 10:00 a.m. the morning after my high school graduation.

And that's how my Penn State story began—before I ever took a college snap—through a steady, by-the-book kind of leadership that felt like an early indoctrination into what it meant to be part of something special.

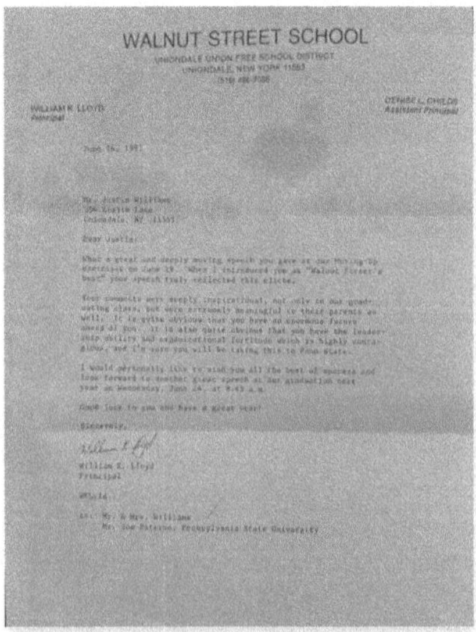
WALNUT STREET SCHOOL
UNIONDALE UNION FREE SCHOOL DISTRICT

Assistant Principal

Dear Justin:

Sincerely,

William K. Lloyd
Principal

Thank you letter for my speech at Walnut Street School.

Show Up and Show Out

THE FIRST THING WE WERE MADE TO DO AFTER FINALLY getting off that bus in front of Holuba Hall—after that Long Island-to-State-College haul—was run the forty-yard dash.

All seven hundred young men who reported for that session had to do it. Twice. And not "twice over the course of the week." Twice right then. Coaches lined us up, stopwatches in hand, and the building buzzed with that nervous energy athletes carried when we all pretended we weren't trying.

After everyone finished, Fran Ganter—the offensive coordinator and running backs coach—called me out.

He made me get up and run it again, one more time, in front of every person in the building. I was the only kid asked to do it. The time was 4.4 seconds, measured by the coaches' stopwatches. In sneakers, not track shoes.

Me with Fran Ganter.

That was my first hour in

Holuba Hall. Right off the bus, before I'd even had time to feel anonymous, I had already separated myself from 700 high school athletes from New York, New Jersey, Connecticut, and Pennsylvania.

I wore my Uniondale High School black mesh cut-off football jersey—gold number 14—with my last name stitched across the back. There was no blending in for me during that four-day camp. That suited me just fine.

I didn't just stumble into speed. I loved track and field. I began competing in eighth grade and by tenth grade I had become a championship sprinter on Long Island. In Nassau and Suffolk Counties, there were roughly ten thousand kids playing varsity football in any given year. About a thousand of them could run a legitimate 4.7 to 4.6—legitimate meaning: flat surface, two times in a row, within a few minutes, in track shoes or sneakers, no funny business. Maybe 100 to 200 could run a real 4.5. And only about ten to twenty could run a true 4.4 or better. From tenth grade on, I was one of those twenty.

So, when Ganter singled me out, it wasn't magic. It was confirmation. In that environment, in that moment, speed was currency—and I walked into camp with a full wallet.

Vintage football photo of me.

That week, I was at the camp as a high school quarterback, and I worked closely with Jim Caldwell. Every day, I threw with him. And anyone who had been lucky enough to stand inside Coach Caldwell's circle—his calm, his command, his way of teaching without ego—knew exactly what I meant when I said he was a great coach and an even better person.

One thing I remembered him telling the quarterbacks was simple and true: if we wanted to be great, we had to love throwing the football. We had to love playing catch. It wasn't just a drill to him. It was joy. And it was obvious he loved throwing and catching with us. That relationship didn't end when camp ended.

Signing My Letter of Intent

THE FOOTBALL RECRUITING PROCESS MADE ME FEEL LIKE AN absolute superstar. And this was *before* ESPN turned National Signing Day into a holiday, before nationally televised high school all-star games, before shoutouts and edits and hype videos living forever on Twitter and Instagram. Back then, the spotlight still found me—but it did it through phone calls, letters, handshakes, and the kind of attention that made an eighteen-year-old feel ten feet tall.

When I signed my letter of intent to play for Joe Paterno and the Pennsylvania State Nittany Lions, Joe "Buddy" Sarra was there. The signing took place in my high school principal's office—formal, quiet, and heavy in the way big moments are heavy. I wore one of my dad's neckties, the kind he wore as a young, promising cricketeer for the Dulwich Sports Club in England.

As I tied that tie that morning—something I had done on my own many times before—I felt something I wasn't expecting: I consciously felt like I was doing something my father could have done but decided against.

My dad had the opportunity to try out for the English national cricket team. In 1970, he was twenty years old, six foot four, about

220 pounds, and he could sprint. He was built to be an overpowering fast bowler—exactly the kind of athlete the British could have used against what was then the most dominant cricket team in the world: the West Indies. His chances were better than average.

But Dad told me that meeting my mother made him decide to settle down and build a life with her instead of taking a chance on sports. I've always believed that if he had gotten a little more push in that athletic direction from my grandparents, he would have gone for it.

And then, of course, I had the obvious follow-up thought: *Where the heck would I be?* (Thanks for NOT playing in the major leagues, Dad!)

That tie wasn't just a tie to me on signing day. It felt like a link—like I could take my dad on the ride he'd had the talent to take at the same age. That morning, I felt the weight of his youthful potential. And I placed that weight, literally, around my neck—not as pressure, but as tribute.

My father didn't just support me; he *showed up*. He never missed my baseball and football games. He gave me more support than he received growing up, so I would never have to feel like I had to trade one dream for another. That was the whole point. I wanted the very best college experience I could have—academically and athletically—and my parents and I believed Penn State, with Joe Paterno, was the only way to go.

That belief mattered more than I understood at eighteen.

Because later—when things started going poorly my redshirt sophomore year (my junior year academically)—I often thought about how differently my story could have gone if I had ended up in a program built on smoke, mirrors, and a recruiting pitch. Had I not chosen so wisely, I shuddered to think what might have become of me once the rough stretch hit.

But before the rough times, there was something else: a period of growth and real potential—and one pinnacle moment in my Penn State career.

In the grand ocean of Penn State football careers, it was a drop. But it was also the kind of moment that most guys who are fortunate enough to strap on shoulder pads for a big-time college football program never get to have.

Why? Because they weren't quite good enough. And the truth was, I lived in that middle space that a lot of "all-this" and "all-that" high school players lived in. I was good enough to play early at a major college program. Good enough to earn a real opportunity.

I just wasn't good enough—long enough—to graduate a starter with the kind of sustained dominance that turns into a clear runway to the NFL. That was the reality.

And it was part of the education Penn State gave me—one I didn't fully understand when I walked into that principal's office, tied my father's tie, and signed my name.

First Quarter

Summer of 1991

I WASN'T INTERESTED IN HIGH SCHOOL GRADUATION PARTIES THE summer of '91. I needed to take some college classes and get back into proper study habits. The second half of my senior year, I dropped advanced placement physics and pre-calculus. What was I killing myself for? I deserved to chill out for twenty weeks. I worked hard up to that point in my life—an honor student who scored 1100 out of 1600 on the SAT in my sophomore year (the first and only time I took it, with no studying and no prep course), rarely getting home from school before 6:30 p.m. since eighth grade because of my commitment to sports, other extracurricular activities, and academics.

I felt entitled to not bust my rear end the latter half of my senior year given that I had accomplished all I could have hoped for. I stayed home from school whenever I wanted those last twenty weeks. Mom or Dad would poke their heads in the room, smirk, then close the door as I lay in bed smiling, hands behind my head, laying on my back. My parents were pretty used to me doing the right thing, I knew. But I also knew, what could they say? I basked in the beauty of being in a position where my loving, but discipline-oriented parents could do nothing but roll their eyes as I cut school.

I didn't want to begin my academic life at Penn State during a hot and heavy fall semester where I would have to deal with not only mechanical engineering classes but a whole new level of football. I felt starting in the summer would ease my transition to college life and make the fall semester flow more smoothly than it would have otherwise. My academic hiatus senior year was deep and broad. Taking my first-class days after graduation was a great move.

When arguably the number one recruiting class in all of America reported to Penn State on July 31, 1991, I was just about finished with freshman English (English 15), an algebra course, and a study skills class. I was on campus at the expense of a freshman summer enrichment program for minority/financially needy students. Buddy Sarra put me in contact with the folks at PSU who were running the program at that time. So, I had already unpacked when my football freshman classmates arrived.

My Penn State wide receiver plaque.

It was a superb feeling knowing the guys I was around during those first freshman-only workouts were, almost universally considered, the highest concentration of top-flight, freshly recruited football talent in the country. And I was a part of that. Expectations were high. And we were all sticking our chests out during drills, sizing up one another. I was the fastest wide receiver in the group, making me the fastest freshman in the class. But the only high school game I ever played receiver was my very last, my all-star game. I had a great deal to learn. There was a highly regarded wideout from Camden, South Carolina, a *Super Prep* magazine All-American, like me. He played receiver in high school, leading his team to a state championship on game fifteen of his senior year. His name is Bobby Engram.

I couldn't believe it when he told me this sometime during those first weeks. The most I ever played in any high school season was nine games out of a possible ten. The differences in high school football in the southern states versus Long Island, New York, are and were glaring. Almost immediately, I became aware of just how far behind I would be in switching from an option quarterback in high school to a wide receiver at the highest level of college football. But JoePa gave me the option to play offense or defense when he recruited me (an honor many do not receive, as I came to learn much later), and I chose offense, simply because I prefer moving forward rather than backpedaling like a defensive back. It was my choice. I had to do what was necessary to make it work.

Just Another All-American

When the upperclassmen arrived for our first full squad meeting, tradition held that each freshman, one at a time, had to stand, state our name, where we're from, and our honors. This happened in front of the entire coaching staff and Joe. I recall that Ki-Jana Carter was the player of the year and the best running back out of Ohio. Michael Archie, my most steadfast roommate during college, was the best running back out of Pennsylvania. Stephen Pitts, another of my most consistent roommates throughout our time in State College, was the best running back from New Jersey. There were many All-Americans in our class. Those of us who rattled on too long about our athletic accolades were rudely and humorously cut off by our older teammates telling us to shut up and sit down.

What was the point of the upperclassmen pretending to care about how good the freshmen were in high school? Nobody cared anymore. I was in a room with many other high school all-stars. High school, as well as the butt-kissing fest that recruiting was for many in the room, was over. I was at the bottom of the barrel, kid. I had a lot to prove.

Early during two-a-day sessions out at the flower gardens, which were out past East Halls and have since been replaced by intramural athletic fields, most of the freshmen got their heads shaved clean after a morning session. Joe wasn't pleased and said so at the end of the afternoon's practice. I managed to escape my scalping, only because my room in Nittany Hall was one of the furthest away from the upperclassmen responsible. There were some hard feelings on the part of a few, but nobody died. Hair follicles sprouted anew, two-a-day practices continued, and life went on. But during the rest of my time in the program, freshmen were not hazed again in such an obvious manner. (You see what I just did there, right?)

I did get to suffer my own indignity soon enough, however. I was performing so poorly in my new position, dropping so many balls thrown my way, that I was excused from practice and sent to an optometrist, who ran every test he could after dilating my pupils. The unfortunate verdict? I had perfect eyesight. I'd like to thank David Daniels '91, a receiver just before I got to campus, for inspiring Joe to try curing my inability to catch by sending me to an eye doctor. Joe did this to great effect with David; he was selected in the third round of the '91 NFL draft. So, David gets drafted, graduates, then I arrive on campus two months later and couldn't catch a cold if someone sneezed phlegm up my nose. It was destiny.

I felt as poorly as I did when I played baseball my first couple of years in America, as a third- and fourth grader: Miserable, down in the dumps, confused, pissed off, and in no condition to joke around about anything and with anyone. But naturally, after getting my eyes checked, I got the business pretty good from O. J. McDuffie '93, Terry Smith '92, and Rick Sayles '93. These were the leaders of our receiving corps; Terry was one of our team's leaders. I took their ribbing personally. On top of that, Bobby was embraced and welcomed into their circle.

From what I could tell, there wasn't a thing to rib Bobby about. His skill and experience at the position were apparent from day one. I'm sure he'd say he experienced some difficulty making the physical transition from high school to Division I, but whatever problems he'd be talking about, they were chump change compared to what I went through. This is the way of things in sports and many areas of life. Nobody cares how old you are or how long you've been around. If you're good enough to contribute, you're in. If you're not, you get the ribs until you can prove your worth.

Ups and Downs of Brotherhood

As camp progressed in August of '91, with the Kickoff Classic in the Meadowlands Arena and our opponent, defending co-national champion Georgia Tech, fast approaching, I felt despondent. Back then, before the email and cell phone era (I feel like a guy born in the 1830s writing that), we had to wait in the lobby of Nittany Hall until it was our turn to call home and/or significant others, sort of like they do in prison. That was what two-a-days felt like, for anyone who hasn't had the pleasure. I sat alone, thinking quite seriously about packing my things and leaving, just as my assigned roommate had done days before, when Penn State legend and seventeen-year NFL veteran Kerry Collins (K. C.) sat down next to me. He was beginning his second year at PSU and must have seen something familiar in my face. Our conversation changed the course of my life. This is not hyperbole or dramatics. It's the truth.

If he hadn't known how I was feeling before he sat down (which I suspect he did), Kerry certainly heard it from me within the first few seconds of our talk. The conversation couldn't have been more than five minutes, and at the end of the first of two weeks of two-a-days. Essentially, he told me he had felt the exact same way the year before and that someone else had made him straighten up and fly right. He recommended that I hang in there, that I wasn't doing nearly as badly as I thought. He went on to say that my malaise was common: Every preseason, a few guys quit, and various others thought about it.

My talk with Kerry left me feeling, suddenly, like I was not the only person in central Pennsylvania who had made a monumental error in choosing to be there. Kerry took a moment to reach out to a teammate in serious need—and he wasn't even waiting to use the phone! I've appreciated it from the moment he got up and walked away. That was almost exactly thirty-four years ago, to the day, as I write this. I still couldn't be more appreciative and humbled. As life teaches me more and more lessons, I've come to understand how easy it would have been for him to be oblivious to my quiet desperation. How often do you genuinely want to hear a detailed response when you casually ask someone, "How ya doin'?"

Kerry and I developed a unique connection during the rest of our time as teammates in Happy Valley. His, as well as our team's magnificent season in '94 ended with an overwhelming performance in January of '95 against the outclassed Ducks of the University of Oregon. One of the few positive memories I have of that amazing time in Penn State football history was driving around Beverly Hills with Kerry in the red Mustang GT convertible we rented. I say "we" because that had been our agreement, but I never paid my share. After we returned from that famous Rose Bowl victory, I didn't get to see Kerry until he came back to campus after his rookie NFL season to spend some money on some of his former teammates. I actually mentioned my debt during that gathering. He looked at me like I had just asked him to deny for the rest of his life that he played football at Penn State. He was a millionaire already, and I was still in college, asking if I could pay him two hundred dollars for a California car rental, while he was paying for drinks for our teammates and me as we celebrated him back in town.

And while I'm writing about stupid things, here's a stupid question I've been asked: Do you think Kerry Collins is racist? You might as well ask me if I think Joe Paterno was a bad football coach. Hopefully, the latter question is as dumb to you as both are to me.

Early in Kerry's pro career, and to my shock, he was labeled with this unfortunate and tragic moniker. For reasons I will go into later, I was neither in contact with Kerry nor did I learn much about the details surrounding the episodes that resulted in the scarlet "R" apparently branded across his metaphoric chest from the media. I have never cared to do too much research because I never personally experienced anything about the man that hinted at him being a racist.

I can say that, coming out of Penn State, he may have been naive about race in America. Who isn't at twenty-two or twenty-three? I understand how easy it can be for a peachy (and I'm talking about his skin color) kid in America, who happens to be great in a sport where 70% of the players are brown-skinned men, to be labeled a racist. I know he's not.

The drunk label is another matter. Kerry has publicly admitted that he was powerless against alcohol early in his NFL career. I believe him when he stated that either alcohol was going to kill him, or he was going to end up in jail. But Kerry's drinking didn't start when he was playing for the Carolina Panthers in his rookie season. Many kids began drinking in high school. Some start serious alcohol consumption in middle school. I have no idea when K. C. had his first drink. I can only comment on the times we were together, drinking, and share some of what occurred.

I am in no way attempting to glorify or justify alcoholism or underage drinking with what I am about to get into. However, you must understand, if you don't already know, that alcohol can become, for many but not all, a big part of life as a college student in general, as well as that of a scholarship athlete in a big-time university setting. It was a regular part of my college experience.

Before I started college, an alcohol binge for me was drinking a few wine coolers with friends either on my birthday, New Year's Eve, or both, depending on the year. During my first summer and fall semesters, I actually attempted to lecture a few teammates on why they shouldn't drink beer, a trite thought now since my indoctrination into binge drinking began the following spring semester as a member of a partnership that ended up being one of my best friendships at Penn State. (More on her later.)

The fact of the matter is that a significant percentage of high-caliber athletes can drink. Quite often, they can drink your average person under the table—way, way under the table. Like, an average dude, a massive majority of the time, stands zero chance of handling the alcohol many of us can consume and then make it home safely. But for many of us in the Penn State football program, consuming many liters of alcohol then making it to a warm bed safely (not necessarily our own), whether by foot, bus, or car, and whether we were driving or not, was routine. I mean, common. As in, it happened all the time. All. The. Time.

It's a situation where sometimes you're responsible about drinking and other times (many times) you were the total opposite—horrendously irresponsible. I am not attempting to condone the wildly inappropriate and darn well dangerous behavior I'm more than insinuating we—Kerry, I, and many, many of our teammates—engaged in. Would I want to know that my own son or daughter had done what we did? Absolutely not. But that's life. And it happens. I threw up once in my life from one to seventeen (of course, not counting the times I'm sure I chucked my guts up as a baby). I was six and sitting between my parents on our couch in South London, England. Between eighteen and twenty-two (my time as a Penn State undergraduate), I threw up at least five times a year. Every single time related to alcohol.

One image that exemplifies what our world was like took place in a house Kerry was renting with another Penn State standout, Kyle Brady. I think it was the end of our preseason camp in '93, our inaugural season in the Big Ten Conference. K. C. and Kyle hosted a massive party. As soon as I got to the house, I was directed to the downstairs, basement-type area where Kyle and Kerry were set up behind a bar with a keg tapped. As I walked in, Kerry saw me and screamed, "You! Get over here!" One thing that receivers always do is listen to the instructions barked out by their quarterback.

When I got to the bar, K. C. told me to open my mouth. When I did, he spit (yes, SPIT) a pretty damn straight, cold line of beer right into my mouth across the bar. I happily swallowed, received my handshakes, chest pounds, ovations, and proceeded to enjoy an extremely fun evening. I actually laugh out loud even now whenever I recall the incident. I'm laughing right now, writing this. These were and are my brothers. I love them, although we haven't seen each other in ages. Still, we're all has-beens now, and the bonds we made are forever.

The last thing I remember from that night was Stephen Pitts and Mike Archie holding me back as a former off-campus roommate—the one who'd stolen my Penn State football gear—showed up at the party without a hint of shame. I was extremely drunk, but didn't ruin the party because my teammates were looking out for me. Most of my time in Joe's program was exemplified by teammates looking out for one another, on and off the field. Many of us still look out for one another to this day. I know we always will. But I wouldn't say that was the case during the '91 season, my freshman year.

An Unsavory Encounter

As I've said, I had a rocky start to my career in the football program. It wasn't made easier by a particular teammate, part of the heart and soul of our team that year. I don't quite recall when, exactly, he and I had the following exchange, but it was no more than a few games into the season. We were in our weight room. I was on a treadmill or a stairmaster machine, positioned on your left as you walked into the room, with the entire room in front of you, much more stretched out in front of you than it was wide. There were mirrors stretching the full length of the room, halfway up the wall from the floor on your right as you walked in, with leg press machines in front of them on the side of the room closest to the entrance, and in front of the machines, I was using to warm up. Upon entering the room, you had to travel a short walkway, take a few steps down a couple of steps, and turn left to the warm-up area.

He walked by and said, "Justin, why are you so unsociable?"

I said something like, "Just not feeling very social." I glanced at him, then looked down at the numbers ticking on the treadmill as I said it, very seriously.

His response was, "Well, fuck you, then," quite deliberate and emphatic. Then he walked away.

That was the first time that teammate had spoken to me one-on-one with no one else around. I was a true freshman, months out of high school. I was having an impossible time imagining being as good as he was. And he was damn good. It was a damn pleasure watching him on the field every day. I looked up to him like you couldn't imagine. I will always have tremendous respect for how talented he was.

My answer to his question thirty-four years ago must have come across the wrong way. I felt like an outsider. I didn't think I was good enough, so I stayed quiet, very quiet, around the locker room and on the field. I thought maybe I wasn't as natural an athlete as the best guys. Things weren't coming as easily to me as they seemed to come to them. I was pissed about that. Furious. Plus, I may have come across as corny. I had a New York vibe, tempered with my British West Indian, suburban Long Island upbringing. I had two parents in my home and an in-ground swimming pool in my backyard. I wasn't a rich kid by the standards of many, but I was well off by the measures of others. I think this had a lot to do with how I was perceived, but as of this writing, I'm not sure.

I was pretty bothered about the exchange, but I wasn't angry. I internalized his behavior, assuming the way he treated me must have been something I'd brought on myself. I was tightly wound, and I *was* and am a bit quirky, in the vein of Kareem Abdul-Jabbar, Grant Hill, or Jim Brown (puh-LEEZ don't think I'm comparing my athletic ability to any of these men!). As I matured in the program, my main nickname became *Dashiki*, due to my Afrocentric take on certain issues that I made quite public in our locker room (like the time I got on the locker room microphone and announced, the day of the O. J. Simpson trial verdict, October 1995, my senior season, "To all you Mark Fuhrman advocates out there, I regret to inform you that The Juice has been found not guilty. That's right, not guilty.") and because I actually wore *dashikis* and went to class often, especially my first two years, displaying my Afrocentric appearance.

I was a serious reader, socially conscious, and not really thinking much about a pro career as I was about taking advantage of the enormous opportunity to be on a prestigious college campus, with no financial worries, able to study whatever I wished. I was trying to figure out how to be "one of the guys" and wasn't doing a good enough job. I bore this teammate no ill will then. I bear him none now. He will be my Penn State football brother until I die. There isn't a thing I wouldn't do for him, nor any of my other brothers, if they asked. But his response was a sign of things to come.

A Classic Kickoff to College

After Kerry's encouragement at the end of our first week of preseason camp that year, I must have managed to impress the coaching staff because I made the travel squad to the Kickoff Classic on August 28, 1991, one of only a few true freshmen to make the trip. Stephen Pitts did too. So did Bobby Engram. Stephen and I made it primarily, I'm sure, because we grew up in the New York City Tri-state area. Bobby made the trip because he'd earned it on the field and posed a real threat to contribute when the game was on the line. And he did.

Still, it was fantastic to be there with friends and family in the stands, only two months after leaving home as a local star with my own legendary moments. It was a feeling of great pride and accomplishment, with more than a little surrealness mixed in, considering that only weeks before, I figured a redshirt was obviously my destiny without question and immediately. But I was wrong. About the immediate part.

Imagine how far my chest was protruding through that well-known all-white road uniform? Imagine being an artist in high school one month, then a few months later standing in the Louvre displaying your work. Imagine playing first violin in your high school orchestra, then, a few months later, warming up to play with the Vienna Philharmonic? Imagine swimming for your high school team, then a few months later, you are preparing to compete for your country in the Olympic Games? My heart pounded, and my senses were on overdrive as I could see my parents and friends.

The game was in Giants Stadium in the Meadowlands, New Jersey, a forty-five-minute trip from my Long Island home—if there's no traffic. Between my childhood home in Uniondale and that professional stadium where I watched the Giants' Super Bowl-winning team in 1986 lies, from west to east, a piece of New Jersey, Manhattan Island, Brooklyn, Queens, and a small sliver of south Nassau County. Interesting fact: Brooklyn and Queens—two of New York City's five boroughs—are located on the same landmass as Nassau and Suffolk Counties: Long Island. It has always amazed me how many people who grow up in this region do not know this. So, I can't expect that you, my glorious reader, would know.

The game took place on a Wednesday summer evening, when the temperature was in the eighties. At University Park, that Tuesday would have required morning classes, a return to our dorms or apartments to change into suits and ties, and then a walk to the Lasch Building locker room near today's Nittany Hall. From there, we boarded our coach buses: the first with all the offensive players and coaches, the second with all the defensive players and coaches. Joe always sat in the first seat on the left, with Fran Ganter directly behind him. I don't remember where I sat on my very first away game trip on a coach bus—probably in the middle somewhere with a window seat—and I know I wouldn't have thought to sit anywhere near the coaches at the front. The rest of the freshmen and I also understood not to sit all the way in the back of the bus, which was reserved for upperclassmen. We were all the best, or among the best, players on our high school teams. We understood how things generally worked when we traveled on buses then.

That four-hour bus trip to the Marriott Hotel in the Meadowlands was somewhat familiar to me, as I had taken it seven times at that point in my life, including for recruiting trips, a visit with my parents, and when my parents and godmother dropped me off to begin my college career. As I write this sentence on August 14, 2025, I've now probably taken the trip to State College from Long Island and back, approaching two hundred times. It's an easy, peaceful, scenic trip that has never gotten old. Regardless of which direction I'm traveling, happiness abounds within my spirit. I love my Long Island 'hood, and I love State College. They are the two places on earth where I feel the most comfortable.

I left campus with a bag packed with a few books, plus an extra shirt, underwear, and socks for the return trip home after the game. A tractor trailer had pulled out the day before, sometime after our forty-five-minute practice (our typical Friday practice preceding a Saturday gameday), loaded with all our football equipment. After that practice, we were responsible for packing helmets, shoulder pads, and any other pads we thought we'd need for the game into big, blue, individual equipment bags. Our shoes were put in for us after the managers polished them.

We waited on the bus for Tom "Viggy" Venturino, head of football operations and regular receiver of a great deal of shit from JoePa for any number of reasons (I state that quite affectionately, because all the players loved Viggy, then and now), to get back on the bus to give us our room keys. For this first game of my college career, as well as the entirety of the '91 and '92 seasons, I roomed with O. J. McDuffie the night before home and away games.

O. J., like most of the guys I played with, was an awesome teammate. He was inquisitive, generous, always open to conversation, and hosted dope parties. One of his best was after the Miami Dolphins selected him as the twenty-fifth pick in the first round of the 1993 NFL Draft. Before reporting for training camp that July, he paid for all the alcohol, including fifty to a hundred forty-ounce bottles of beer. I drank three in about an hour. The next morning, I decided it was prudent to spend brunch at the hospital. I know damn well I had alcohol poisoning, but I certainly wasn't going to report that. A few other teammates who had been at the same party put our heads together and decided we would tell the doctors we ate at the same place and that we thought we got food poisoning. After that third forty-ounce, I didn't recall a thing that happened until I woke up, naked, alone, in a pool of vomit I could not immediately move out of; I was so sick. I've joked with O. J. and many others about this and many other moments we shared together. We are all exceptionally glad there were no camera phones or social media to make us think such events needed documenting.

Standing on that field in Giants' Stadium, going through our pregame drills, with my family watching, was awesome. It was the very first time I wore those mostly white uniforms and helmet, and black turf shoes, rather than cleats. Back in August 1991, turf fields were largely like carpets rolled over concrete arena floors. There were a couple of layers of whatever underneath, but it was not enough to soften any falls. Holuba Hall on our campus was similar, except the turf there was bristly, so if I hit the ground and slid across it with exposed skin, the top layer of my skin came off, producing what is referred to as strawberries or turf burns. These little bundles of joy hurt the worst in the shower. And we didn't have gentle showers. For some absurd reason, our locker room showers in the Lasch Building jetted out what I describe as a harsh and irritating mist. While we could adjust the angle of the spray, we couldn't control its intensity, and the sharp stream hit like salt on a turf burn. SMH!

We handily beat the defending co-national champs. They didn't score a touchdown until the game was decided, even if the 34–22 final makes it look closer than it was. That was because Joe took out our first teamers and started emptying the bench to give backups, third-stringers, and sometimes fourth-stringers a chance to play. Like many guys who played for Joe, we felt that was a contributing factor as to why it was so much harder for us to contend for national championships.

Long before the current playoff system, the margin of victory was a key determinant in who would be named national champions in Division I college football. Joe refused to run up the score against opponents, unlike other coaches. Of course, I now agree that Joe's stance was correct to take. He preferred not to win championships if embarrassing other teams and their coaches was a prerequisite. During that time in college football, Joe felt that winning as many games as possible with a bunch of young men who worked hard, didn't take any shortcuts on or off the field, while carrying themselves with class and confidence—that was the aim. I've been a varsity football head coach. What goes around comes around. Treat others the way you'd like to be treated.

Ups and Downs of a Winning Season

The week after beating Georgia Tech in the opening college football game of the 1991 season, we walloped Cincinnati 81–0. I never saw Joe so apologetic after a football game. He was genuinely embarrassed that we scored what remains the most lopsided victory in modern college football history between two Division I teams.

It's really hard to put up that many points against other young men standing in front of you, trying to stop you. In high school, my Uniondale Knights won our homecoming game in my junior year 54–0, so I understood what it was like to be on the winning side of a blowout. But that Cincinnati game was crazy. Joe played every single person he could possibly play. Backups to the backups were on the field the entire fourth quarter, and we still scored. J. T. Morris, one of the few true freshmen who did not redshirt that year, scored two long touchdowns (runs of over fifty yards) on inside runs (plays designated between our offensive line's left and right tackles).

I distinctly remember one of them being a fullback dive play right up the gut, or attacking the middle, the center of the defense. Our offensive game-calling got that vanilla. I think the only way we could have stopped scoring was if Joe told the quarterback to take a knee four times in a row. Of course, that would have been even more humiliating to them, so we kept scoring, much to Joe's chagrin. The point is, you must be pretty good to score that many points against any team at that level of play. And our Penn State team was damn good.

And no, I didn't play in the game. There was no doubt afterward that the intention was for me to redshirt, but I was the only redshirt that year who traveled and dressed for every regular season game, including our bowl game. Joe later admitted in a press conference that he "darn near" played me that season, which made me fully understand why I only played on the foreign team (redshirts typically spend the season pretending to be the other team during practices) for two days my entire career at PSU.

It was the week we played West Virginia, our ninth game of the season. My quarterbacking days in high school made me a perfect candidate to try to outmaneuver our stellar defense, one that gave up 167 points during the regular season (our offense scored almost three times as much that same season). Our defensive coaches were wary enough of Darren Studstill, their athletic, run-oriented quarterback who split time with the pocket-sitting Jake Kelchner, to get me off the offensive field for the week. During my entire tenure in the program, I never felt worse physically than I did after the Tuesday and Wednesday practices that week.

Imagine: I had to run option plays for our first- and second-team defenses. If you are a major Nittany Lion football fan, I'm sure you can recall some of the superb players, guys who couldn't wait to get their hands on me. Who were the starters I competed against that week, who I remember most often ending up on top of me, sometimes as I was belly up, sometimes face down? Tyoka Jackson, Lee Rubin, Keith Goganious, Darren Perry, Leonard Humphries, Mark D'Anofrio, and Lou Benfatti. Then there were our backups, many of whom were basically starters, guys like Jeff Kerwin, Phil Yeboah-Kodie, Marlon Forbes, Rich McKenzie, Vin Stewart, Willie Smith, and Brian Gelzheiser. All these guys knew I was there to run the ball. If I somehow got four yards, I'd have to run the play again, to the same side. Fun! It ends up, though, that I did my job well. Pride and competitiveness quickly kicked in. I was on a scholarship, too. We beat the Mountaineers 51-6.

Expectations were as high as they could be in 1991. Penn State was still an independent university, not affiliated with any athletic conference. We knew the wins had to pile up in order to be considered for a national championship. Because the national champion was decided by votes then, we knew that even a single loss would almost certainly eliminate us from championship contention. We had an air about us, where we felt we could beat anybody, and we had the right combination of players on both sides of the ball to make it happen.

The fifth year seniors on the 1991 team, guys like Terry Smith (current PSU associate head coach) Lou Benfatti, Tony Sacca, Keith Gogainous, Mark D'Onofrio, Al Golden, and Sam Gash were true freshman fall of 1987, the season after our program's storied national championship victory over Heisman Trophy winner Vinny Testaverde (who was never the same for the rest of his football life after that five-interception game in January 1987), Michael Irvin and Coach Jimmy Johnson, an earlier and more legendary version of the University of Miami football team. That PSU senior class began its tenure as freshmen with expectations of accomplishing the same goal. They saw, as upstarts in the program, the ramifications of a championship season. When you get a taste of that sort of thing, you only want more of it.

During the '91 season, it was clear to my freshman class that those seniors expected to produce a national championship season. It was going to be their time, finally. The Hurricanes were going to be yet another obstacle to overcome on our schedule that season. But not before we faced another storied football program. Two of the three loudest games I ever experienced as a player happened during that season. The USC game was the first.

My First Time in Southern California

Three games into the season, we faced the Trojans of the University of Southern California. I consider this game the inaugural away game of my college career since the Meadowlands felt like a home game because Nittany Nation has a huge alumni base in New York City and New Jersey. This was the first time experiencing the to-the-minute travel itineraries always coordinated by the ever-present Tom Venturino, director of football operations, or "Viggy" as he is affectionately known among our brotherhood. This guy worked some serious overtime for Joe and the program and did so for decades.

We left campus for Harrisburg, PA, on Friday, September 13. We had to ride coach buses to an airport there because University Park Airport isn't large enough to handle the big jets necessary for a cross-country trip with the formidable load of a big-time college football program like Penn State's. I suppose many people would see this drive as a bit of a hassle. For me, fresh out of high school? It just added to the fun. I was like an avid golfer on an all-you-can-pack-in-the-shopping-cart free shopping spree at the local PGA Super Store. I couldn't believe I was going, though I don't think I exuded any outward manifestations of how excited I was. There were a lot of older guys on that team who knew how to conduct themselves like champions. In our program, you learned fast, "Act like you've been there before."

It was formative for my fellow freshmen and the sophomores to be around upperclassmen who, with precision, manifested the qualities Coach Paterno wanted in his football players. The '94 season hovered in the distance, and our group was to become the nucleus of that very fine, record-setting team. The seniors on the '91 team laid the foundation for the '94 season. Good programs and organizations continue to benefit from this dynamic. Success breeds more success. And Joe focused on doing it all with honor.

I have a few visceral recollections from that trip. I remember waking up that Saturday morning, early at 5:30 a.m. Pacific time, and walking out onto the balcony area connected to my room. The temperatures bordered on hot. The smog over Los Angeles was a living, breathing organism. Taking in my first conscientious, deep breaths on the West Coast of the United States, I thought, "*Wow! The air is thick*!" The game wasn't until early evening, and the day stretched before me.

I was completely absorbed by the bus ride from our hotel to the Los Angeles Coliseum. The realization that I was about to step into that stadium—the site of the 1988 Olympic Games—felt surreal. I was a serious competitor and a devoted track-and-field fan back then, so approaching the place where Carl Lewis captured four gold medals, matching a feat accomplished only once before by Jesse Owens in Berlin in 1936, filled me with awe. That history was alive for me as we pulled closer.

As we drew closer to the stadium, I was struck by the condition of the surrounding neighborhoods. It wasn't something I expected, and it stayed with me. Traveling with the program, I would see versions of this again and again, slowly beginning to understand the real estate realities of building massive sports arenas—especially in urban areas. When we watch events like the Los Angeles or Paris 2024 Olympics on television, we're swept up in the spectacle and the grandeur.

Rarely do we think about the homes and buildings just beyond the camera's frame. I know I never did—until that moment.

I remember driving on Crenshaw Boulevard, famous because of movies that deeply affected my sensibilities as a young African American man. Films like *Boyz n the Hood* (1991) and *Menace II Society* (1993), as well as early-nineties West Coast hip-hop artists like Eazy-E, Dr. Dre, Ice-T, and Ice Cube, appealed to my developing sensibilities about African American manhood. At their essence, there was nothing "gangsta" about these films or these artists. They represented (and still do, unfortunately) depictions of life inside the urban Black American experience, so very foreign to so many.

It was difficult for my eighteen-year-old mind's eye to accept that the Olympic Games were hosted within what was essentially South Central Los Angeles, depicted in media I consumed to that point as one of the most notoriously violent and poverty-stricken places in our country. Make no mistake, the Los Angeles Coliseum is dead in the middle of "The 'Hood." It was my introduction to a deeper self-examination, a reckoning with the intersections of my identity: full-scholarship Penn State football player, British West Indian New Yorker, suburban-raised kid, English major, dark-skinned male in mostly white classrooms. This wasn't the only way the inequalities inherent in our lives as Americans would become apparent during my undergraduate years.

Another searing memory from that fall '91 West Coast visit to play the Trojans was how difficult it was to stay focused on the field for our pregame routine. The stadium's big screens and audio system blasted the history of every great running back ever to play at the University of Southern California. And, as if that wasn't enough with which to contend, there was the USC marching band. They were set up *on our sideline* in tight formation, blaring every note of every famous song having anything at all to do with Trojan lore. My gosh, I can still hear it now as I type these words. *BAAAAAAAAAA ba-ba-ba BA BA BAAAA buh BAAAAAAAAAAA*! Damn, was I pissed. I know I wasn't the only one. Their behavior was obnoxious, lacking in etiquette, and just plain disrespectful.

The Trojans had produced a stinker of a game two weeks prior in their opener against Memphis State, losing 24–10. Their coach, Larry Smith, admitted that it may very well have been the low point in USC football history to that point. They had an extra week to prepare for us, and they were revved up, very emotional, and determined to erase the previous game's humiliation from their fans' palates. Which was precisely what they did. We lost 21–10.

They blitzed us mercilessly and often, much of the time right up the middle. We fumbled the ball seven times, losing it twice. Tony Sacca threw two interceptions and was sacked five times. In relief, Matt Nardolillo threw another pick. The same USC defender caught them all. From beginning to end, those 65,000 fans were some of the loudest I've ever experienced. I just couldn't believe it. Everyone in that stadium—fans, players, coaches, the band, and the beer guys and gals—was on a mission. We were not up for the challenge. That game on that day was, for me, the definition of what playing in your home stadium was all about. Never again did I take the phrase "home field advantage" lightly.

Losing to USC was deflating. I remember the exhaustion almost more than the game itself—two hours on a bus, five hours on a plane, then another bus to the hotel, crossing two time zones only to spend half the day waiting to play a nationally televised game we would lose. Afterward, I showered, pulled my suit and tie back on, boarded another bus to the airport, flew five hours, rode two more hours by bus, crossed two time zones again, and finally walked back to my apartment sometime after 3 a.m. Sunday morning, starving, with nothing to eat until the dining hall at Pollock Commons opened. I slept a few hours—maybe more—until I could drag myself to brunch. If I were banged up, I still had to see the trainers for treatment, instead of doing what I wanted most: resting all day, maybe watching some NFL, before pulling myself together for classes and practice on Monday.

Two years from the publication of this book, during the 2028 Penn State football season, the team is scheduled to travel early in the season to Syracuse, Michigan State, and Nebraska, three weeks in a row, before a late-in-the-season visit to the USC Trojans. Although today's players are making a lot more than twenty-six dollars a week (our cash payment received each Friday during the season for weekend food) and have access to food twenty-four hours a day, seven days a week, winning a football game after a lengthy trip is still very difficult. That proved true more than I would have liked during my Penn State career.

After licking our wounds from the USC game, we rattled off three consecutive wins against Brigham Young University (BYU) and Boston College at home, as well as Temple University at the University of Pennsylvania's historic Franklin Field. I had been on the field at that arena three times before, competing as a sprinter for my high school track team at the iconic Penn Relays. Then it was time for us to visit the University of Miami, the second-ranked team in all the land, against us, ranked ninth. We were full of confidence. We believed intensely that we would win that game.

Conflict in Coral Gables

After we arrived at the hotel on Friday, two of my high school classmates, who were beginning their college experience at the University of Miami, came to see me. Only months earlier, we wore our black-and-gold caps and gowns, graduating on the front lawn of Uniondale High School in Long Island, New York. By then, we were part of a big-time college experience—and one of the biggest college football games in America that weekend. I was dressed in a suit and tie, feeling an unexpected sense of calm with friends I'd known since third and seventh grade. At the same time, there was a surreal brush with celebrity that had settled in after spending six games on the sideline in uniform with Penn State. This would be the seventh game of my college career. It was Saturday, October 12, 1991.

Going into the contest, with a 5–1 record, Coach Paterno had stated to the media, "We're not anywhere near as good as I had hoped at this stage. It's because we're careless. Right now, we're not playing with a lot of poise."

According to my dictionary app, poise means "a dignified, self-confident manner or bearing; composure; steadiness; stability." This word, along with various other words, phrases, and statements, entered my lexicon during my time playing for Coach Paterno. Like any good teacher, he rattled them off to us repeatedly. Sometimes warmly, thoughtfully. Sometimes with bite. So would his assistant coaches, many of whom played for him. It could be said that the Penn State culture at that time was built around those words, phrases, and statements. It all added up to who Joe wanted us to be, not just during games, but for the rest of our lives.

For whatever reason, during coach bus trips away or blue bus trips to Beaver Stadium on campus, from that season and for the remaining four, I secured the third seat on the left as you entered the bus. Joe always sat in the first seat on the left, Fran Ganter right behind him, then me, always by the window. I never had a consistent seatmate, but I had that spot. I wanted to be as close to Joe as possible, whenever I could, so I could learn as much as I could about him. How often do any of us get to be in the consistent presence of a person considered to be an icon in their field? I wasn't going to let that opportunity pass without immersing myself as fully as I could in who that man was. I was all in in terms of what he was selling, how he carried himself, what he stood for. I still am.

So, it was one of the biggest shocks of my life witnessing how Miami fans treated Joe the second we got off the bus to walk into the Orange Bowl, the Hurricanes' home stadium, where they were in the midst of a forty-game winning streak. As we stopped, the crowd swarmed around the door, quickly forming a human tunnel that was about five people deep on both sides and stretching like a gauntlet way further than should have been allowed. This tunnel was just wide enough for us to walk two by two, shoulder to shoulder. I was right behind Coach.

"Fuck you, Paterno! You fucking stink! We're going to fucking kill you today!" This was the general gist of the abuse being hurled at us.

Inside, I was stunned by the abuse I was walking through, most of it aimed at the same man who had once sat with my parents in the den of our home in Uniondale, back when I had already been committed to play for him for six months. I was going to be a Penn

Stater whether he showed up that day or not. Now, here he was, being viciously cussed out right in front of me. Why?

Maybe it had something to do with the last time my Nittany Lions faced the Hurricanes—January 1987, the national championship game, still the most-watched college football game in history. Most of you reading this already know how that one ended. For Hurricanes fans, the rematch they'd been waiting for had finally arrived. They were loaded for bear.

We finally made it into the visitors' locker room. As was our custom, whether home or away, we put our bags down and turned around immediately to go out to the field to gain a feel for the conditions before getting fully dressed for the fight. At home, we took our pregame walk around the field in half our uniform. Away, we'd wear our jackets and ties. As I hit the field, I was surprised by two things: the sandy base of the field and the four Miami fans in the upper deck of the Orange Bowl who were screaming bloody murder at Joe. At one point, I noticed him glancing up at them and smiling. I realized then that Coach wasn't taking any of the abuse personally, like I was. I had more growing up to do.

Reasons why we lost? They brought much more energy and passion to the field than we did that day. Additionally, we weren't solid on special teams, as we gave up a long punt return for a touchdown, returned from their own nine-yard line. And Miami had five receivers on their roster who were at least six feet one inch tall. We had a total of three defensive backs who were six foot one, none taller, and none of them played in that game. In the second half, three of Miami's touchdown plays took off the clock less than sixty seconds. One was the ninety-one-yard punt return; the others were eighty and forty-two-yard passes to starting receivers who were both over six feet tall.

The final score was 26–20. Our QB1, Tony Sacca, who was drafted in the second round of the 1992 draft, threw for 263 yards and two touchdowns. He was sacked eight times. Miami was penalized eleven times for 124 yards. Both teams were utterly exhausted when the final whistle blew.

It was a typically hot day under the South Florida sun, and the game was a fight to the final play—relentless and fiercely competitive. None of us wearing those plain white jerseys and pants, blue numbers, and black shoes had come to Penn State to play for Joe Paterno and accept losses like that. It stings when you expect to win and don't.

The locker room, the buses, and the long flight home gave us plenty of time to study the faces of our teammates, coaches, and support staff. I didn't see any quit in anyone after that brutal defeat. We didn't lose again the rest of the season.

One of my favorite philosophical statements I learned from Joe is: "You're never as good as you think you are when you win, and you're never as bad as you think you are when you lose." Truer words have rarely been spoken.

Freshman Year Ends with a Crescendo

The rest of the way, we outscored our opponents 244–80, including overwhelming performances against the Fighting Irish of Notre Dame at home (21–0 at the end of the first quarter in route to a 35–13 decimation) and the University of Tennessee at the Fiesta Bowl (42–17, with a second half offensive and defensive explosion that made America remember that Penn State really loves playing football in southern Arizona). During my time at dear ol' State, we won four of five bowl games. At the end of my freshman football campaign, I learned, in very great, painful detail, why Coach Paterno remains the all-time leader in bowl game wins for a D1 college coach (24).

After classes ended during the '91 fall semester, my teammates and I didn't get to go home after the last final exam. Unlike the majority of the 40,000 undergrads who jetted out of town to enjoy a month off from school before returning for the spring semester, our reward for earning an appearance in a January 1 bowl game was hard work. Joe worked us relentlessly during that time, every year I was an undergrad. We always had back-to-back two-a-day practices in full pads, with lots of food, sleep, and position meetings to study film of our upcoming opponent, as well as film from the previous practices to analyze what we were individually doing well and where we each needed to improve.

I don't remember if we got to go home that December for a few days before having to take a chartered flight to Arizona. When you go to five bowl games in five years, many of the trip details blend together in the mind. Plus, the bowl experiences of my first two years had some differences from the last three, explained by the difference between being an independent school ('91–'92) versus a Big Ten school ('93–'95). Due to a delay in Harrisburg, Pennsylvania, we arrived in Phoenix an hour later than expected the evening of December 26, 1991. We had our first practice in southern Arizona the next day. Joe was on record saying that Friday, December 27, practice was a big waste of time. We were sloppy and lethargic that first day. He was extremely concerned and ripped into us pretty good. The first half of the actual game reflected this first practice in the Southwest.

Although down 10–7 at the half, we fortunately had seasoned players on both sides of the ball, as well as a deeply experienced coaching staff and head coach. This combination can often push the right buttons and make the necessary plays to produce a come-from-behind win against an opponent working hard to secure a staple victory in the annals of its program. The pinnacle example of such a victory during my time in the program was our victory over the Fighting Illini on their field during the fall of '94. More on that later.

The Fiesta Bowl was my favorite of the five bowl games we participated in. The Rose Bowl was a close second. The reason? Women. I will never forget pulling up to a southwestern outdoor BBQ food joint that was one of the official functions organized by the bowl game organizers for our team and our opponents, the University of Tennessee players. A local person got on the bus and handed out cards to each player, numbered from one to over a hundred. We were told there were women inside with numbers matching ours. Our task was to find the one who shared our number. The morning after our victory, the team was pulling out of the JW Marriott Scottsdale Camelback Inn Resort & Spa early to catch our flight back to Harrisburg. All I can tell you is I got zero sleep that entire night. My roommate, Mike Archie, and I left two women in our shared room as we hustled out to get on our offensive team bus. I ended up flying back to Arizona in April 1996 to spend some time with one of the ladies I'd met during the Fiesta Bowl trip in December of '91 and January '92. I never had more fun during a bowl trip.

In the weeks leading up to that trip, Mike and I decided to room together. At that time, we were still living with the freshman football teammates Joe had assigned to us. Jeff Hartings and I had spent our first fall semester as student-athletes at PSU living together. We decided to go our separate ways for the bowl game. I will always be very glad Joe bunked Jeff and me together during our freshman year. It was the first time in my life that I got to live with a "white" dude, and I assume it was the first time he got to live with a "black" guy. We got along fine. His first college girlfriend turned out to be one of the best friends I've ever had. She is a "white" girl from a town near Binghampton, New York. Jeff and Mike grew up about four hours' drive from each other, both from small towns, and both are pretty reserved guys. I was raised in densely populated suburbs of London and New York City. Although I do know how to be reserved, I am not so by nature. I am a people person. I love connecting with people, and love a quality conversation about any number of things. Yet, Mike and I had a bit more in common.

We got along so well and had such a good time during our Fiesta Bowl trip that Mike and I ended up roommates on campus from sophomore year until we graduated. I love Mike. Like tons of people who grow up in the middle of America, he was raised in a small town. In his case, western Pennsylvania, not far from the Ohio border. In college, Mike and I listened to a lot of the same music (hip-hop and R&B) and were devout followers of the television show *Martin*, starring Martin Lawrence. Additionally, we loved playing video games (he a bit more than I), especially NCAA football. Before all that, though, we were two teammates in southern Arizona, enjoying the fact that we were on scholarship at Penn State, playing football for Joe freakin' Paterno. We made each other laugh—a lot.

One of the highlight comedic moments occurred as he and I walked away from our hotel room, heading to the pep rally. This was a day or two before the big game. Mike, as was his habit, wore a baseball cap. I don't recall if he was wearing it backwards or if it still had a tag hanging off it. Or both things may have been true. We were not even thinking about how we looked, other than the fact that we had no facial hair, as per Joe's orders.

My roommate Mike Archie (l), me (c), and his childhood friend Billy Jackson (r), in our undergraduate years.

We were shooting the breeze, taking in the sights and sounds, when special teams coach Tom "Scrap" Bradley, walking in the same direction but far enough away that he had to yell, said, "Hey Archie, take that hat off, you're not in the ghetto anymore!"

My jaw dropped. Half disturbed, half facetiously, I said, "What the fuck did he just say?"

"Wait, wait, it gets better." Mike was setting me up for the kill shot. "He recruited me!"

"Nooooooo fucking waaaaaaaay," I said, as we both started howling with laughter.

As I think of this moment, thirty-four years ago, I remember it vividly. It was such a stupid, ignorant thing to say, let alone yell with other people around. But as we approached our first bowl game experience, as we were having the time of our lives in southern Arizona, months from our nineteenth birthdays, we were already well aware of the penchant some of our "white" elders had for having little clue of how to appropriately address us. Then and now, it would be easy to head down a rabbit hole of analysis as to why Scrap felt at ease shouting what he said. I've never asked him about it. Archie was one of the most coveted running backs coming out of high school in the state of Pennsylvania. Scrap was known as a fabulous recruiter of western Pennsylvania talent. More than anything else, Mike and I just found his comment hilarious. I feel like that's the moment we decided we would be roommates again if the chance presented itself.

Movin' On Up

THE GENERAL RULE WAS THAT FRESHMEN BALL PLAYERS LIVED in dorm rooms in Pollock Commons (an undergraduate dormitory complex within walking distance to the football training facilities) during their first year. After that, we were moved into Nittany Apartments (which are, essentially, the same distance to our practice facilities), generally reserved for select and fortunate upperclassmen in the general undergraduate student population. Those first two semesters of our Penn State experience really did facilitate making friends outside of the football fraternity. For whatever reason, Jeff Hartings and I were transferred out of the dorm during the second semester of our freshman year and moved into Nittany Apartments with Bucky Greeley and Geff Kerwin, guys I immediately liked very much. Bucky was always smiling and jovial. He would eventually become the anchor of one of the greatest offensive lines in the history of college football.

Geff was a defensive back from Kearny, New Jersey. He was a tough Italian kid who gave me hell in fall '91, the one week I played foreign team quarterback to help us prepare for West Virginia's offense. He was cool as hell as a roommate, but didn't smile as much as I expected he would/should, given his coolness factor. We talked about the similarities and differences in our backgrounds. His was more challenging than mine. He passed away on October 24, 2013, at the age of forty-one, which was also his jersey number at State. I've missed him since the day he transferred from PSU. His death will hurt me forever.

Geff and I never went partying together, never studied together, and didn't have any mutual connections besides Bucky. We had just a few conversations in our apartment, but they always left me wanting to know more. I should have asked my questions. Maybe I assumed there would always be time. Hartings and I were freshmen, still dealing with mandatory study halls on Monday through Thursday evenings. Geff and Bucky were sophomores. We lived in upper-classmen housing, a significant step up from the dorms. I believe we were the only two freshmen who only lived in the dorms for a semester. Regardless, when you have the opportunity to get to know someone, especially when they are really different from you, jump at the chance. Geff is the only teammate I lived with whom I feel I didn't give myself a chance to get to know. He wasn't easy, but I could have done more.

Since meeting and losing Geff, I listen to my inner voice now when it tells me to reach out to someone. It's made an enormous difference in my life. In this way, Geff Kerwin, number 41, will always be with me.

Second Quarter

Sophomore Year

After returning from a successful and super fun Fiesta Bowl in January 1992, I got to visit home for a bit before the start of the new semester. The spring semester of 1992 began only a couple of weeks after we got back to State College from the bowl win. It was to be my third semester at Penn State, counting the six-week summer session I attended only three days after my high school graduation during the summer of '91. By that point, things at home were pretty good from my perspective, only because my mom was keeping her cancer diagnosis to herself. Even my dad didn't know. So, after that spring semester, I decided to spend the summer at home, the only summer I elected to be home during my undergraduate years.

Through connections with the football program, I gained what I thought was only an interview for an internship with Merrill Lynch, based in the World Financial Center, downtown Manhattan, New York City. As it turned out, there were about 150 interns that summer. Only two of us had our own offices: the son of the president of the Manhattan branch and yours truly. My office, with a gorgeous view of the Hudson River and the surrounding area, which made me a little ill because it was so high, was one of two locations for me that summer. The other location was a few blocks uptown. I took a company shuttle between the two locations when necessary. Unlike most of the other interns that summer, I actually did real work. Because they knew I was an English major, they had me writing descriptions for in-house professional development classes offered to the thousands of employees within the Tri-state area (New York, New Jersey, Connecticut). I met with administrators when I needed additional information or when I had completed particular write-ups. This was a paid internship, too. I would have stuck with it more than six weeks if 1) my paychecks were getting to me on time and 2) if it didn't take me an hour and a half to get to and from downtown Manhattan from my Uniondale home.

That internship was a valuable experience. For the first time in my life, I commuted on the Long Island Railroad and the New York City subway every day, in a suit and tie, to go to work in what was an impressive sea of humanity. Although this was another notch on my ever-increasing list of significant accomplishments, it wasn't treated as an enormous deal in my home. I don't remember telling any of my childhood friends that I had a paid internship in the city. As usual, my accomplishments were taken in stride.

Compared to what I know now as an educator of twenty-seven years, back then, I was clueless about how big a deal it was and still is to have a paid summer internship as a college student in one of the chief financial epicenters in the world, let alone having my own office within that experience. Ultimately, though, I couldn't see myself dealing with that commute every day, for twenty or thirty years, like one of my immediate supervisors (her commute was an hour longer than mine!). And though the view from my office was spectacular, I didn't get to interact with people as often as I wanted.

My Second College Season Begins

Getting my workouts in after the nightly commute back from Manhattan during the summer of '92 was brutal. That strain was a big reason I walked away from my Merrill Lynch internship—it was jeopardizing my ability to show up at Penn State in August ready to pass our running test. Fourteen forty-yard sprints. I was in the fastest group, alongside Ki-Jana and a handful of others. We had to make the time—4.9 seconds or better—on thirteen of them, with only thirty seconds of rest between runs. The rest clock started the second you crossed the line, and you had to jog back to the start. By the fourth sprint, your legs were heavy and your lungs were on fire. You might get five seconds of stillness before exploding forward again, chasing the line and the clock, over and over.

This test simulated a fourteen-play drive in a game. The closest I ever came to missing a rep during this test was in August '92. It didn't look like it to those watching (the entire team, all the coaches, and Joe), but I knew what was going on in my head. I never ran slower than 4.9 seconds in any run over the four years. I took that test under our masterful strength-and-conditioning coach, John Thomas. I also never dared to go home again for the summer. Staying in State

College and working out with my teammates was the way to ensure that the test was a regular day's work for me.

Coming out of preseason two-a-day camp (two full-contact practices per day, something that is no longer legal in college football), I earned the powder-blue practice jersey given to an offensive starter at Penn State. I was quite proud. Knowing all the legends who had come before, playing on the same fields, for the same head coach, it was an enormous honor to be given the jersey, wearing it alongside Bobby Engram, O. J. McDuffie, and Tisen Thomas for what would turn out to be the entire season. I had reached the top of the mountain, being named a starter at Penn State, playing for a legend, Joe Paterno. How many young men would have given anything to live that life? It was a genuine thrill, and time to step up and be counted on the field of play.

That season turned out to include amazing personal highs, overshadowed by a staggering tale of a talented team that collapsed.

Great Start to the Season

We opened with Cincinnati, their second year playing D1. Unlike the previous season, where we put up a final score of 81–0, routing a team that was clearly not ready to make the jump to top-level college football, our trip to Cincy to kick of the 1992 season was a much tighter affair. We escaped with a 24–20 victory, a serious warning sign of things to come.

Half-jokingly, I will say that Joe always tried to put the fear of God in us about the first game of any season. He'd always tell us that you never really knew exactly what kind of team you had until you played a few games. His biggest concern for game one, though, was always special teams and turnovers.

At the highest levels in college football, you can do a lot to simulate situations and the feelings you get in games, but there is no substitute for what happens on game day. Back then, we recognized that we hit in practice more than most other teams in the country. Tuesday and Wednesday practices during the season were tough. Maybe Joe cut a few minutes off those practices towards the end of some seasons, but then our bowl game preparation would revert back to preseason two-a-day practice sessions, where we were hitting every day.

This became so central to our mental and physical conditioning that many of my teammates who transitioned to the NFL would come back to campus during downtime of their rookie years to report that the lack of hitting in NFL practices made them feel uncomfortable, if not unprepared, for games. I stopped coaching football after the fall 2014 season (I was the head coach at Uniondale High School, my alma mater) because I wasn't comfortable adapting to the modern methods of teaching tackling and the transitioning away from the very physical practices I felt made us at Penn State better than most. However, I absolutely understand that the sport had to respond to the deep concerns about the brain health of the men and boys who play the sport.

After overwhelming Temple 49–8 in Beaver Stadium, my "welcome to college football" moment occurred the following week against an overmatched Eastern Michigan team we beat 52–7. During the first half, John Sacca, our starting QB1 to open that season, called a go-route for me in the huddle. This meant someone on the sideline intentionally called a deep pass to me. Given what I know now, I wouldn't bet any money at all that offensive coordinator Fran Ganter called my number of his own accord.

Either Jim Caldwell, our quarterbacks coach, suggested the play call, or Coach Paterno made the call himself. Throughout my time wearing those beautifully simple uniforms, I watched Joe regularly snatch away Fran's play-calling responsibilities. During the '92 and '93 seasons especially, I was regularly one of two or three guys who ran in the play calls from the sideline to the huddle on the field. Sometimes Joe would grab me and give me a play to run in while Fran gave Phil Collins a play to run in. Often, Joe would be giving me a play call from the '82 or '86 teams. In exasperation, Fran would translate the old play Joe wanted to run into the current nomenclature, and I'd sprint in to give John the play. Whenever Joe got a feeling in his gut or in many clutch situations, he was absolutely in control, not Fran Ganter or anyone else. Joe was usually on the money.

As I lined up on the right side of our offensive formation, we were around our own fifteen or twenty-yard line with the tunnel to enter the field behind us. Getting myself ready, I noticed that I had one defender on me, playing off about five yards, with no one behind him—man-to-man coverage. They tried to stop our run game and had eight or maybe even nine defenders "in the box," meaning between our offensive tackles and within five yards of the line of scrimmage. We had the perfect call, as long as we could protect John long enough to allow him to take five steps after receiving the snap, so he could throw it downfield to me. That was exactly what happened.

I exploded off the line and sprinted past the corner back (CB) by the time I was fifteen yards off the line of scrimmage. Around twenty-five yards deep, I looked up and back for the ball. It came down to me in a perfect spiral. I had beaten the CB bad enough that I didn't have to catch the ball over my shoulder. I actually had to slow down, opening my left shoulder to turn to catch the ball. John had slightly misjudged my speed. But the forty-nine-yard completion was good enough for a major change in our field position. A nice start to my career.

Next up was Maryland, whom we beat handily 49–13. Then came Rutgers at Giants Stadium, whom we beat 38–24. By the end of that game, playing opposite O. J. McDuffie and alternating snaps with Tisen Thomas as we rotated in plays for John, I was leading the team in average yards per catch.

Even though I didn't have nearly the number of catches that O. J. had, it was still a pretty awesome accomplishment. I didn't get caught up in thinking about how good I was though. Quite the contrary, I felt like I lived a privileged existence. I was surrounded by a really high concentration of guys who were gifted athletically, interestingly varied in intelligence, had enough discipline to be successful student-athletes, and were funny and fun as hell. I was all those things as well. And then I became a regular, heavy contributor. I stayed focused on the next play. Plays turned into quarters, quarters turned into games, games turned into days, days turned into another practice, and another day of classes and schoolwork.

Schoolwork. Now there's a term you hardly hear anymore regarding the young men who participate in the two college sports that turn a tidy profit: football and men's basketball.

School and Coeds, Not Necessarily in That Order

Playing football at Penn State was hard in the days before paid players and a playoff system in which the national champion is decided on the field, not by the opinions of sports reporters prone to biases for or against certain coaches and/or programs. One big reason? We had to go to class. An article published in 2011, almost exactly a year before Coach Paterno was relieved of his coaching duties, proved that even at the end of his career, Joe was still a catalyst for a spectacular graduation rate for his players.

Being caught missing classes was worse than missing breakfast or dinner, crimes that resulted in a mandatory and debilitating 5 a.m. workout. By the time I arrived on campus in late June 1991, stories of players missing buses to away games were described in mythical terms, as if such a disaster could occur only with the simultaneous sighting of a unicorn galloping past the chicken coops between Nittany Apartments and the natatorium. Being in Joe's doghouse was the inevitable result of doing anything described here. One would be barking up the wrong tree, spending time in Joe's crosshairs. He had absolutely no tolerance for stupid questions from the media and these sorts of self-inflicted wounds by his players. If he couldn't trust you, you were not going to play.

Did he treat everyone the same way or fairly? He told us all the time that he knew he couldn't. I think he clearly cut me more slack when I started playing poorly than he would have if I were many other guys. I didn't realize this until well after my playing days were over. Kenny Jackson, my position coach from '93-'95, told me various times how much Joe liked me. Others reinforced this idea. So, I would sometimes go to Herculean lengths to make it to breakfast on time. Girls and alcohol were usually the reasons I almost missed a few breakfasts.

Being a football player at a major college football program like Penn State made it easy to meet women. I was an English major, so I knew how to communicate, and how to listen. Throughout my life, I've had more close female friends than male friends. This probably had to do with the fact that my mother and father had more sisters than brothers. That and, well, I was a momma's boy growing up. My parents taught me to respect my mother and sister. I always put the toilet seat down when finished, never talked back to my mother (except that one time!), and was required to take my sister out to dinner and a movie the day I got my driver's license. My mom taught me how to slow dance with a woman, how to talk—and, more importantly, how to listen—and she helped me understand that women often see the world differently than men. One time when I was home on a college break, I sat with my mom in our den watching something on TV. Out of the blue, she turned and said, "You know she loves you."

"What?"

"Kristine*. She loves you. Please be careful. She is lovely."

I was taken aback. It was the first and only time my mother spoke to me so earnestly regarding a woman. I sometimes brought home friends from Penn State, almost all of them raised outside of New York. We traveled into the city to see Times Square, the Empire State

Building, and the Statue of Liberty (which was under construction/renovations during those years).

Kristine met my parents at my home, too. She became a nurse, like my mom. My mom was six years older than my dad. Kristine was six years older than me. We met in my freshman year. She was beautiful, intelligent, and my tutor. Until she made her feelings clear, I had no idea she liked me that way. We dated throughout my undergraduate years. I was serious about Kristine, but not serious enough.

I put her through more suffering than anyone deserves. Unwilling to fully commit to her, I was more concerned with being free to do what I wanted, when I wanted. Yet I was too selfish and too in love to let her go completely. Kristine revealed to me the otherworldly gravity, the sheer force of a woman's unadulterated love and the lengths she would go for you, to you, and with you when her love, this love, was aimed squarely at your entire being. Talk about overwhelming and intoxicating. I was not ready, nor was I worthy. I will always harbor sorrow and shame for breaking her heart.

I learned so much from her. I have apologized to her. But sometimes apologies just do not cut it.

I got to a point where I could call on multiple women on any given night for companionship. Early in my college life, I did. Often. During my last couple of years, although the options remained, I chose to be alone more often. I learned that companionship without friendship was your favorite dish, improperly heated and seasoned. When I started college, I assumed I would find a woman I could marry by my twenty-first birthday. This was when my dad married my mom. However, I became increasingly confused about how to select a life partner. Fortunately, I had various platonic female friends.

I met Sandra (Sandy) Zurner in my first fall semester while living in Hartranft Hall in Pollock Commons. She was dating my roommate, Jeff Hartings, so we only spoke in passing. By spring semester '92, their partnership had run its course, and somehow, Sandy and I started hanging out. Between her and my teammate, Vin Stewart, I gained substantial and repeated experience in the ancient art of how to throw up due to binge drinking. Usually, the spring semester evenings of bingeing would start later (the study hall for all freshman athletes on campus ended at 9 p.m., Monday to Thursday) or, shockingly, even by the standards of the day, in the early afternoon on weekends.

Sandy was pretty essential to my development into the sort of person my parents and I ultimately wanted me to be. During that spring, summer, and fall, I took courses that eventually satisfied my minor in Black Studies (African American Studies, as other universities refer to it). Sociology introduced me to oppression and its debilitating effects. My Black Studies courses explored the twentieth-century struggle for equality among African Americans, and my Education Theory and Policy classes revealed how schools often reinforced racist, sexist, and classist ways of being.

During my free time, to deepen my contextual understanding, I read historical texts such as *Black Reconstruction in America* by my intellectual hero, W. E. B. Du Bois, *Before the Mayflower* by Lerone Bennett Jr., and *They Came Before Columbus* by Ivan Van Sertima. That year, I left classes regularly, very upset. I pieced together my own family history, how my ancestors, on both sides of my family, were enslaved on the island of Barbados, and how that destroyed my family's ability to trace our deepest origins back to Africa. Later in my life, it kicked in that I am descended from the strongest Africans—those who survived the unspeakable horrors suffered in the putrid hulls of British slave ships; those who endured the humiliations of the auction blocks; those who did not die in the brutal Caribbean fields before somehow passing to me their unbreakable DNA.

In 1992, as a sophomore at Penn State, I grappled daily with this knowledge intellectually, emotionally, and spiritually. My mom told me sometime after I graduated and before she died that she had genuine concerns that I might become radicalized by my growing Afrocentric sensibilities. My nickname, *Dashiki*, given to me by Kenny Jackson, my position coach, hadn't come out of thin air.

Despite being angry at the "white" world for the sins of too many of its foremothers and forefathers, every day, as I listened to my answering machine after a day of study and workouts, Sandy's voice rang out with an update of what she was doing, where she expected us to meet up, and with whom, in the near future. I wanted to be mad at her, too. But I couldn't. She was too much fun, completely accepting of who I was and who I was becoming. We'd have heavy talks, then go out and get very drunk in various frat houses and apartments downtown. We'd hit up these spots, make our way to the kegs, and quickly end up being in control of beer distribution, only to ensure we never saw the bottom of our cups. I never came close to drinking Sandy under the table, then or whenever we've been able to connect since. When I went too far, which was too often, she made sure that, if I had a mandatory breakfast and/or a 6 a.m. workout, I would be there.

During school breaks, Sandy came to my home in Uniondale and met my parents. I went to her home in Endwell, New York, to meet her family. Her dad was an English teacher and a sports coach, exactly what I ended up being. She attended my mother's funeral. Our friendship has also survived divorce, the death of her father, the mental illness of our siblings, distance, time, and many other things.

Relationships like ours are not particular to Penn State. However, when we say, "We are Penn State," friendships like ours are part of what we mean. Our world cannot have enough friendships like this one.

I saw Desiree Trader-Kent for the first time in February 1992 at the Paul Robeson Cultural Center. I was sitting in the audience watching various African American coeds in costume playing different African queens from history. Desiree played Queen Nzingha. By that fall, we were cool enough that I could call her well after midnight, sometimes waking her up, so I could sleep on her floor when my roommate Mike Archie had company. She lived in Nittany Apartments, too, so it was super convenient.

I love Desiree because we are very similar in very specific ways (she will laugh while she reads this paragraph). We are the sort of "black people" who are "too black" for most of our work colleagues and/or "white friends," yet not "black" enough, but tolerable in many "black" circles. Our sense of humor is relatively disturbing to people of various complexions. And we don't care. We march to our own beat, and we're very cozy in our own skins. We can spend very long stretches in silence and/or solitude and be perfectly fine. My family has spent long weekends at her home because her house is much more awesome than mine (I should have earned a science degree). When you click with someone and your gut tells you to remain in their orbit at all costs, follow instructions. It's made all the difference in my life.

*Not her actual name

The Hurricanes Blow Away Our Season

The first game of my college career that I knew I was the official starting receiver (flanker or "x" designation in our play calls) along with the great O. J. McDuffie (split end or "z" designation in our play calls), was our home game against the University of Miami, Saturday, October 10, 1992. Both teams were undefeated. We were ranked #7 in the country; they were ranked #2.

As we walked off the practice field at the end of our Thursday practice, quarterbacks coach Jim Caldwell got even with my right elbow and told me I would start. I never thought much about why it was Jim who told me and not Fran Ganter, the offensive coordinator or Jamie Barresi, the receivers coach at the time. I was glad it was Jim, though. He was the guy who drove my parents and me around State College on August 2, 1990, making them feel very comfortable sending me to Penn State. He was also the guy I worked with at the quarterback position during the PSU football camp in June 1990, in preparation for my high school senior season and eventual Super Prep All-American.

On Friday evenings of home games, the starters and backups took our famous blue buses from the Lasch building to the Toftrees Golf Resort Hotel in State College. This was to ensure we got a good night's sleep and were not distracted by friends and family in town for the Saturday game. Whether home or away on Friday nights, I roomed with O. J. that season.

It meant a lot to spend that kind of time with him during his senior season. Watching him in practice every day—alongside so many other players on both offense and defense who would go on to the NFL—was an education in what it truly meant to be an elite football player. The longer I stayed in Penn State's program, the more future pros I practiced with and against, hung out with, and came to know well. Being surrounded by that level of talent, I couldn't help but believe I might one day play on Sundays too.

Being on the field against those Hurricanes felt surreal. It was also a culmination of events that dated back at least to January 1987, when I watched Joe and the boys beat a star-studded Hurricane team in the national championship game, securing a legend-defining victory. Our contest would be the second game we played against them since that win. We had lost to them in Coral Gables during the '91 season. We wanted revenge. And we were confident.

Throughout the week, and especially during similar weeks when we were playing a marquee matchup, our offensive game plans became simpler. Coach Paterno's tried-and-true philosophy was to run the football on offense, keep our defense and their offense off the field, control the line of scrimmage on both sides of the ball, and play tough, disciplined defense. In these games, he always focused on making sure we knew what we were doing by keeping things as simple as possible while reminding us, usually right before we took the field, to play worry-free, and bring some swag.

The rest of each week in practice was spent focused on being precise, decisive, tough, fast, poised, and disciplined. All week, as I looked over at the preparation conducted on the defensive field, it looked like we were preparing for Miami's passing attack more than anything else. We expected them to throw the ball all over Beaver Stadium. They surprised us by going against type and pounding the ball all game between the tackles—a factor in their victory. I didn't sleep much the night before the Miami game. I had in my stomach a nervous feeling that didn't settle until kickoff. Coach Barresi came to our room to quickly go over the play scripts for our opening offensive series.

Even though it was my first start of the season, I don't think anyone looked at it as a big deal because usually, Tisen Thomas was in on the first play, and I ran in the second play. For the Miami game, our roles were reversed. Tisen was dealing with knee issues, which helped open the door for me to earn more trust from the offensive coaches. I felt bad for Tisen. He was struggling to compete but was pushing through. Like so many others, he was an excellent teammate. We did our two mandatory weight workouts together each week. He made every exercise supremely competitive between us. At the time, I didn't realize that he was showing me how seriously to take my preparation. Before the arrival of our head strength and conditioning coach John Thomas, Chet Fuhrman was responsible for our conditioning. Things were really loosey goosey with our weight workouts before J. T.'s arrival. Tisen showed me there were no shortcuts for us, even if others took them.

During our first offensive series, I had my only catch of the game. The play call was "Louis split 97." The first two terms presented the formation. O. J. and I were to line up on the left side of the formation, with him on the outside and on the line of scrimmage to my left. I was in the slot position between him and our left tackle, Greg Huntington. The running backs, Brian O'Neal and Richie Anderson, were split, each lined up behind our quarterback, John Sacca, and five yards behind our two offensive guards, John Gerak and Mike Malinowski.

The "97" designation explained the protection and the receiver routes. The "9" meant maximum protection for John, meaning everyone was staying in to protect John except O. J. and me. The "7" directed O. J. to run a six-yard hitch or stop pattern, while I run a ten-yard flag route, or a forty-five-degree out pattern where I look over my left shoulder for the ball. John was required to read the defender covering O. J. If he backed up, O. J. would be thrown the ball. If he stayed tight on O. J., the ball would be thrown behind and over the head of the defender to me.

The immortal college football play-by-play broadcaster, Keith Jackson, said my full name and hometown immediately after my catch. On the broadcast, Bob Griese praised the play as a well-placed throw by John and a sure-handed catch by me. The game is on YouTube, and the catch occurs at 12:00 into the recording. I wish I had other opportunities to make plays during the game. Maybe it could have changed the outcome. I know for certain that I was under-utilized not only during that game but throughout that season. We were too reliant on O. J. and Richie, our starting tailback. This glaring flaw in our offensive philosophy was exploited by defenses throughout the remainder of the season.

Although we lost the game 17–14, the stadium was rocking the entire game. I think this was the first game in Beaver Stadium history where hip-hop music was played during our pregame routine. I remember a lot of us being pleasantly surprised. During this time, a shift was occurring at PSU. More than ever before, "black" culture was being overtly embraced and not just in the Beaver Stadium music selection. There was a small section of "black" hair products in McClanahan's, the clothing, apparel, and merchandise store on the corner of College Avenue and South Garner Street, which every single person who has ever attended classes at the University Park campus is very aware. The music stores where we could purchase CDs for our players were selling more and more hip-hop artists. All of this was an enormous deal for the African American players.

It's miserable when you lose a ball game you fully expect to win. There was significant internal turmoil and fallout as a result of this loss. In the short term, I don't think Joe supported us as well as he could have. But in the long run, the moves he made took us steadily towards that glorious 1994 season, his final undefeated team, and the last PSU football team to achieve a perfect season. I don't think the '94 season happens unless the incoming classes of '90–'92 experienced that '92 season.

The Collapse After Miami

THE FOLLOWING WEEK, WE LOST AT HOME TO BOSTON COLLEGE 35–32 against a well-coached Tom Coughlin team, the same guy who went on to coach two Super Bowl-winning New York Giants teams with Chad Powers, otherwise known as Eli Manning, at quarterback. We were ranked ninth; they were ranked twentieth. We hadn't awakened from the heavy fog we fell into after the previous week's loss until the fourth quarter of the BC game, too little too late. But what happened at Toftrees before the game not only sealed BC's victory but also our season.

As we walked into the dining room for breakfast, getting settled ahead of the noon kickoff, a few guys didn't carry the edge Joe expected. They were laughing, caught up in their own conversation. One of them was Reggie Givens—one of our captains.

Joe was furious. He tore into Reggie in a way that left the room stunned—demeaning, public, and uncomfortable to watch. Looking back, that was the moment Joe lost the team. I've never spoken to anyone from that group who sees it differently. I've also been told that Joe believed it was the only team he ever lost to.

Much of my '91 class feels to this day that the upperclassmen spit the bit after we lost to Miami. Going into the season, the goal was a national championship. Back then, the feeling was that we would never have a championship bestowed upon us by the sports writers with a loss on our record. So, our aim was to win every game. After losing to Miami, we felt that many of the upperclassmen decided the season was over; there was nothing else to play for.

PSU football lettermen Reggie Givens (r), Shelly Hammonds (c), and me (l) posing at Beaver Stadium.

We went two and three in the final five games of the season, including a season-ending loss in the Blockbuster Bowl (remember Blockbuster Video?) against a Stanford University team coached by the legendary Bill Walsh, an NFL Hall of Famer who coached the San Francisco 49ers to three Super Bowl victories in the 1980s with Hall of Famers Joe Montana, Steve Young, Jerry Rice, Fred Dean, Charles Haley, and Ronnie Lott.

I met Ronnie Lott during his last season (1994) in the NFL, when he played for the New York Jets, and practiced at Hofstra University at the time, part of which is in my hometown. Richie Anderson, who was drafted by the Jets during the '93 draft, brought me onto the field in July, right before my return to Penn State to start our legendary season. He also got me into the locker room to meet Lott, running back Curtis Martin, and many others. I socialized with them at a local hangout called Buttles, named after its owner, Greg Buttle, a Penn State and New York Jets great.

We also lost to Brigham Young University (BYU), coached for almost thirty years by LaVell Edwards, and Notre Dame, coached by Lou Holtz. Our last three losses of the season came on the road against great coaches.

Standout Moments

A FEW THINGS WILL ALWAYS STAY WITH ME ABOUT THE TRIP OUT to Provo, Utah, to play BYU. Cougar Stadium, as it was known in '92, before it was renamed LaVell Edwards Stadium in 2000, stands at an elevation of over 4,500 feet above sea level, which was (and is) a serious concern for visiting teams, since the thinner air can negatively affect player performance. Joe spent time convincing us that there was nothing to the altitude. Still, I distinctly recall feeling like I was gasping for air during pregame warm-ups—and I was in the best shape of my life. I know I wasn't the only one who felt that way. Some of us looked at each other, our eyes wide, as if to say, "Why the hell am I feeling like this? Are you? Didn't Joe tell us this altitude stuff is all poppycock?"

Whether the glorious view of the Wasatch Mountains and the altitude were figments of our collective imaginations or not, by half-time we were down 27–3 en route to a 30–17 loss. Richie Anderson and O. J. McDuffie scored touchdowns, and I caught a two-point conversion from Kerry Collins, who passed for over 300 yards. He threw a long ball to me in the end zone, but it was knocked out of my hands by one of their defensive backs. Their offense ran the ball fifty-five times out of a total of seventy-four plays. They dominated us up front. Of the fourteen offensive linemen on BYU's roster that season, half of them were at least 290 pounds. Eleven of them were listed at six foot five or taller. I never felt like we were in that game.

Another interesting note about this game was that Joe made the trip an educational experience for the team. After the loss, we stayed an extra night in Salt Lake City, which led to an experience few non-Mormons ever have. The next morning, we were guests of honor for a private performance by the Mormon Tabernacle Choir during our visit to Temple Square and the Mormon Temple. But that night, a few of us left the hotel and found a club within walking distance. One thing led to another, and a few ladies ended up back at our hotel. I'll let you fill in the rest. The trip wasn't a total loss.

As we pulled up to the temple, we learned that the Family History Library, the largest research center for human genealogy in the world, was across the street. I was wowed to learn that Alex Haley did much of his research there for his powerful, semi-autobiographical, historical fiction novel *Roots: The Saga of an American Family* (1976). The following year, ABC adapted this novel into a TV series of the same name that broke records with 130 million viewers. As a kid growing up in New York, most people I knew watched that miniseries, which seemed to air annually in the eighties, probably around Black History Month. Little did I know that I would see with my own eyes the library where Haley did some of his research for a story that captivated me as well as much of America. This moment was even more meaningful to me because during the summer of '92, I had read *The Autobiography of Malcolm X* (1965), on which Malcolm X and Haley collaborated. I had no idea there could be an intersection between my love of American history, specifically as it related to the inclusion of Black people, and a visit to the Mormon Temple. Unfortunately, before we flew home, there was an occurrence that offended a few African American members of our team.

It just so happened that our football team were not the only guests of honor of the Tabernacle Choir that day. There were African dignitaries seated in the temple along with us. We all sat and listened to the choir sing a montage of songs celebrating the culture and history of the American South. While the choir expressed how much they wished we were all in Dixie, some of us sat there, absorbing the moment. Older teammates like Lee Rubin, who became a captain during the '93 season, his roommate Shelly Hammonds, known to us as "The Boston Strangla" because of the crazy stats he put up against that team over multiple games, and Tyoka Jackson, or "Mr. Sackman," a well-earned moniker denoting his penchant for burying quarterbacks from his defensive end position, led the way in their anger at the tenor and tone of this show, which was focused on us, while ignoring the presence of leaders from the African continent. Those three guys in particular, were unapologetically Afrocentric in their thinking. Ty grew up in Maryland, the doorway to the South. He was actually an extra in the film *Glory* (1989), starring Denzel Washington, Morgan Freeman, and Matthew Broderick, which concerns the first Black military unit commissioned by the United States government during the Civil War, the Fifty-fourth Massachusetts Infantry Regiment. Shelly grew up in South Carolina, the Deep South. All of us were raised to be extremely uncomfortable in that moment.

Back home in State College, when Joe found out how we felt about the event, he was immediately apologetic. But then he realized that apologizing only to a couple of older African American players wouldn't be enough. The broader context was that he had berated Reggie Givens, a heavily respected team captain, a guy who always left everything he had on the field, and a guy who happened to have brown skin. To this day, Reggie regularly returns to campus for games and letterman weekends. He is, and always has been, a lifer. He absolutely was not the guy to undress the way Joe had. Joe lost a lot of respect in the eyes of a significant number of his players, no matter their complexions. He knew it.

When he learned that his planned event, where a core of "black" players, most of them underclassmen, were made to feel extremely uncomfortable, Joe recognized that he could not blow the moment. He needed to build for the future. The most significant outcome of all this was that, for the rest of the season, Joe met only with the Black players on Sunday mornings in our players' lounge. Here's a summary of what Joe communicated to us:

"Guys, first, I apologize for that rendition. I wasn't aware they were going to do that on our behalf, and I wasn't aware that African leaders would be present and playing second fiddle to us. Once you brought it to my attention, I immediately understood why you guys would feel the way you do. I apologize, okay?

"Look, I am very aware of how difficult it is for each of you to be on this campus." Noticing some doubt in some of our faces, "Hey, now wait a second. You think it was easy for me to have this Brooklyn accent and this face at Brown University in the late 1940s? I took my share, guys. I have an idea of what you guys go through here. I've done my best to surround you guys with great people who will support you in ways you need. And I will continue to do that. The kind of experience each of you is having here is important to me. I want you to continue to develop yourselves, and not just athletically. Penn State has a lot to offer you guys, and you guys have a lot to offer Penn State. Take full advantage of the opportunities you've earned here. I care about you guys a lot. I am always available to you."

What did it mean to be "black" at Penn State in the early 1990s? Wally Richardson, our quarterback in 1995, being repeatedly called a nigger during answering machine phone calls after losses. Having no place within walking distance of campus to get our hair cut or purchase products we preferred for our hair and skin. Having no place to eat that simulated, in any way, our home cooking. Having very few professors or graduate assistant instructors who looked like us. Regularly meeting "white" coeds who had never seen a "black" person before their arrival at Penn State as students. The color change that would occur at the McDonald's on College Avenue every Friday and/or Saturday night during the fall and spring semesters between two and three in the morning. "White" customers dominated the seating area and lines to get food, as all the parties and bars, per Pennsylvania law, would shut down at 2 a.m. I often sat and watched as the "black" students, coming from wherever we were partying, would begin taking over the food lines and sitting area as the "white" kids began to trickle away. By 3 a.m., there was rarely a "white" student left. These are some of the broader strokes of being us that Coach Paterno said he had some understanding of.

As usual, whether on the sideline during games, in the locker room during pre- or post-game talks and prayers, or during any bus ride, I tried to be as physically close to Joe as possible. It was vital to me to learn as much as I could from him. During these talks, I always sat on the floor next to Joe, either directly in front of him or slightly to one side. I didn't want to miss a word. He regained our trust with these meetings, and our hopes for a positive future at Penn State. Coach Paterno became human to me, to us, as the '92 season crumbled under the weight of massive expectations and blown opportunities.

His ability to take responsibility, to apologize, to extend himself, to show some vulnerability, was exceedingly impressive for a guy who by that point was very much a living legend. I couldn't believe he could connect with us the way he did. Separated by multiple generations, by outright lies telling us he was a different race than us, by wealth, fame, and prestige, it was still vital to him to connect *with* us. It's one of the many lessons I learned from him, up close and personal, that settled deep inside me.

The week after the trip to BYU, we had to prepare to face Notre Dame, as everything else that was happening to us continued. The visiting locker room was unnecessarily tiny, like annoyingly tiny. But that was the point, right? It snowed, with snow accumulating on the field. This made it difficult to play a ball game. We only completed seven of twenty-eight passes on the way to losing 17–16. It was a tight ball game that we lost on the last play. Eventual Hall of Famer Jerome Bettis shook hands with as many of us as he could as we walked off the field. He had respect for his opponent that day. They ran the ball just a little bit better than we did. Bettis and Reggie Brooks were the reasons why. Once momentum turns against you, getting back on course can be difficult.

I didn't have a catch in that game nor the bowl game against Stanford. We made it easy for Bill Walsh. They played eight men in the box regularly to defend Richie Anderson, Brian O'Neal, and our run game while double-teaming O. J.'s receiver position. My position was left one-on-one versus their cornerback, something our coaches refused to try to exploit. Besides the Hall of Famer on the sideline for Stanford, it also had one on the field, free safety John Lynch.

We were beaten that season by high-caliber coaches and teams. However, we should have done better than 7–5 for the season.

My Pinnacle Game as a Lion

While playing sports at a high level, you learn how to compete the right way. One of the things you learned to do, especially at Penn State under Joe Paterno, was to play hard and not take plays off. You practiced how to remain focused and disciplined throughout an entire practice, so you would do it for an entire game. On October 24, 1992, against the University of West Virginia, I put together my most complete, satisfying game. Part of being able to have this sort of game was having your coaches trust you enough to call your number. I only had two catches, one in the first quarter and one in the fourth, but both were extremely impactful to the game's outcome.

The first catch, ironically, was almost the identical play call for the only catch I had in the Miami game that we lost in a close battle two weeks earlier: "Louis split zip 97."

In the Miami game, we had started on our half of the field, our own 38-yard line. Against the Mountaineers, we were deep in their side of the field, just nine yards from the end zone. O. J. lined up on the left side of the offense, and I lined up on the right.

The play called for me to shift toward O. J. before our quarterback, Kerry Collins, received the ball from our center. This motion accomplished a few things. First, if my movement towards O. J. was mirrored by one player on the Mountaineer defense, this would reveal that they were in man-to-man and not zone coverage. This early or pre-snap information would help Kerry decide whether he was going to throw the ball to me, O. J., or make another decision based on how much time he felt he had before he would be sacked. Second, my motion disguised the fact that we ran the same play, to the same side, against Miami.

When the ball was snapped, O. J. was supposed to run six yards and hitch or stop, turning to expect a pass from Kerry. I would push a few yards into the end zone, then break at a 45-degree angle left, aiming for the back corner of the end zone. The rest of the play was built around protection. The offensive line, running backs, and tight end stayed in to block, giving Kerry as much time as possible to make his decision. Only O. J. and I ran routes. We were Kerry's only targets.

As we lined up, Kerry, O. J. and I, as well as Joe and our offensive coaches on the field as well as those seated high above the field in the press box, saw that they were playing zone coverage. My motion across the formation made this observation clear, since no one in their defensive backfield shifted across with me. We ran the play. Kerry had time to wait for me to come open since two guys jumped on O. J.'s route. I caught the ball towards the back of the end zone, with no one near me. Every one of my teammates came to celebrate with me in the end zone, which was appropriate. I wouldn't have been able to score if even one of them didn't do their job. In the video, you don't see that O. J. got to me first. You do see Richie Anderson (number 20), who cut my hair a few times while we were teammates, and with whom I ended up hanging out in my hometown when he was drafted by the New York Jets after this season ended. Richie played for the Jets for ten seasons. Because of him, I got to meet two NFL Hall of Famers in the Jets Hofstra University locker room, legendary free safety Ronnie Lott (during his final season in the league) and Richie's fellow running back, Curtis Martin. You see my roommate for a semester and starting center, Bucky Greeley (number 60), take an extra beat with me to enjoy the moment. Bucky and I continue to communicate almost daily in a group chat I started with a core group of my teammates from the '94 season. Troy Drayton (number 18) and Brian O'Neal (number 29), you see as well, are great players and people. You don't see me being dapped up by the guy who threw me the ball, but Kerry Collins (number 12) was right in there, too. It's gratifying for me to have him be the quarterback during my best game. This moment may not have occurred if a year earlier in Nittany Hall, he hadn't stopped to let me know everything would be okay. Whenever I play the lotto, I play the numbers of these and other teammates with whom I felt the closest. It's okay if I never win. Having the time I had with those guys, in our prime—I'm already a winner.

In the fourth quarter, with the score tied at 26–26 and about three minutes left, we faced a crucial third down deep in our own territory. I carried the play call into Kerry. I don't remember whether it came from Fran Ganter or Joe, only that the play was designed for me.

I lined up on the left side of the formation, with our tight end, Troy Drayton, positioned closer to me than usual instead of next to the offensive line. That alignment was meant to stretch the defense and create confusion. The play also included a fake handoff to Richie Anderson, who had been running the ball well all day, to draw the defense forward just long enough.

My job was to sell a short route—take a few hard steps, make the defender believe the ball was coming quickly—then turn and sprint past him. When he bit on the fake, I took off. All I had to do then was look up. Kerry delivered the ball perfectly, and the pass went for forty yards.

We finished that drive with a touchdown, a score that finally put the game out of West Virginia's reach.

On the offensive team bus immediately after the game. I sat next to O. J., listening to Coach Don Nehlen's post-game press conference while we ate the boxed snack we were given for the three-hour ride home. Coach Nehlen explained that my second catch in the game broke their backs. The volume was loud; everyone on the bus could clearly hear. O. J. tapped me on the leg, nodded, and gave me a big smile. I smiled back. This acknowledgment from an opposing head coach, as well as from my great teammate and fellow receiver, was everything.

Since it had been a 3:30 p.m. game, we got back home in time to quickly hit the town and soak up some fruits from our labor. Some of my teammates and I ended up in Players for a few hours, one of our favorite spots. It tended to be a target-rich environment, shall we say. There would have been a longer than usual line that night, in anticipation of our late arrival. My boys and I wouldn't have to wait in line, though.

It's been said—and written—that the 1994 Penn State football team might be the last Nittany Lion squad to finish a season unbeaten *and* untied. If that turns out to be true, I'll say this much: We were a collection of young men determined to pay whatever price was asked of us, or asked *by* us, on or off the field, to achieve perfection. Early in the season, we decided we wouldn't go out during the week. Saturdays were for business; Saturday nights were for celebrating the work that earned it.

Joe made sure of something else: every day at dinner, we sat with a different group of teammates. And after a while, something rare and beautiful happened: This became the only team I've ever been part of where I felt completely comfortable sitting with *any* guy and talking about *anything*. Thirty years later, that feeling remains.

There were no bad practices. There were no bad teammates. Everyone counted. Everyone *mattered*. Starter, backup, scout team—it didn't matter. Every man showed up ready, focused, and committed. For one season, regardless of your class year, hometown, complexion, faith, or place on the depth chart, everyone was equal.

Sometimes you love people you don't like. Sometimes the reverse is true. But the 1994 team taught me the extraordinary power present when every last member of an organization pulled in the same direction, at the same time, for the same amount of time—no matter what.

These days, many of us are still in touch, usually in group texts that have nothing to do with the '94 season. If we *do* bring it up, our reflections always end with the same truth: We were unflappable and unbreakable.

By Joe's standards for evaluating teams, we've also turned out to be an exceptionally high percentage of quality human beings. "Winning and losing are fleeting impostors," he'd say. It's the trials and tribulations required to make winning possible—that's what forges the permanent bonds. More than most, my teammates and I willingly endured the required suffering. We learned to revel in it. To smile in its face.

Because by 1994, we knew what it felt like to be broken. In 1992, the program *was* broken. In 1993, we rebuilt ourselves by getting comfortable with discomfort—in the weight room, on the field, and in our own minds. We were pushed to the breaking point, over and over, and then asked to take a few more steps past that point. And we did, until being broken became part of life, normal, nothing to fear. Dr. John Thomas, our strength and conditioning coach? Brother, we're still talking about you. There is no "us" without you. You were a vital piston in the engine that drove us to be men.

At some point, as a team, we just stopped being afraid—afraid of throwing up, of looking foolish, of not finishing, of not impressing, of not meeting expectations, of failure. We stopped giving a damn about anything except giving everything for the brother next to us. And we believed, whole-heartedly, that Joe knew what he was doing in bringing us all together and making us pay the high price of being a Penn State football player at that time, in that era.

That's how we won them all in '94.

We didn't know it then, but everything we endured—the breaking, the rebuilding, the choosing each other again and again—was preparing us for what came next.

Third Quarter

Either You Get Better or You Get Worse

After the 1992 season, my redshirt freshman year (my sophomore year academically), I brimmed with potential, determination, excitement, and vigor. I was a crucial member of one of the most recognized college football teams in America. I had scored my first touchdown, started in nationally televised games, came through in clutch situations, and decided on an academic major. My present and future as an athlete, a person, and an academic crystallized before me. What happened to me was a continuation of who I had been and a precursor to who I was going to be.

Like a great many of my teammates, I thoroughly enjoyed the relationships I forged with people who had nothing to do with (and more often than you might think, wanted nothing at all to do with) Joe's team or his program. During the early 1990s at Penn State, the process of football players gaining experiences beyond the dominant football experience began almost immediately, by design.

Sometime in the eighties, upperclassmen suggested to Joe that he allow them to live among the student body rather than be isolated throughout their undergraduate and college football careers. They felt that, although the special treatment was nice, it made it difficult to have moments where you could, if you really wanted to, feel like a regular student on campus. It was important to those guys that the players who followed them be afforded the chance to have a more rounded college experience.

So, my first fall semester ('91) I lived in Hartranft Hall in Pollock Commons. My first football roommate was Jeff Hartings, who later won two Super Bowls with the Pittsburgh Steelers. Jeff was "The Standard" at every level he played, meaning he was the yardstick against which all other linemen around him were measured. During that first fall, our freshman year, he was injured and had to have knee surgery. He got around on crutches and, understandably, was not feeling too good about himself, while I suited up for every home and away game.

I remember getting back to our dorm room after a road game. Sometimes, he'd be sleeping. Other times, he'd be studying. On a Saturday night. In a big-time college football environment. We won many games that year. He should have been up to risky business. But he was never that kind of guy. He was majoring in economics and on the brink of becoming a three-year starter, an academic all-American, and an NFL All-Pro.

I'll always be extremely proud to have spent quality time in Jeff Hartings's immediate presence. He left me with a few things I've carried ever since. The athletic, academic, and familial success he's realized since our freshman fall has been no accident. He's an extremely devout man who would tell you, very sincerely, that all he has accomplished is based on his faith. I would humbly add that Jeff, like many young men who often chose to be a part of Joe's "Grand Experiment," embodied all the attributes for which Penn State football players under Joe Paterno were known: toughness, discipline, intelligence, poise, fundamentally sound, powerful (not just strong), and relentless. I was all those things too. Additionally, many of us were spiritually devoted to the biblical God, a devotion that manifested in different ways. Some of us studied the Bible together through the Athletes in Action campus organization founded by Reverand Tim McGill in 1979. I did not. Before Penn State, I had a deep connection with the Bible and my faith.

Losing Faith While Discovering My Path

Joe and I both attended private religious schools. I was a student at Saint Joseph's Convent in London, England, a boys' school run by nuns, from 1977 to October 1980, between the ages of four and seven. I was scared every single day. The environment was high academic pressure for sure. But by the time my parents withdrew me to move to America, just before my eighth birthday, I could write in neat cursive, knew my multiplication tables by heart up to twelve, had begun learning to play the recorder, and had been exposed to the French language. It was an amazing academic foundation, but the combination of corporal punishment and prayer at least four times a day, along with Bible study, literally put the fear of a largely scary God deep inside of me. It wasn't until I was a student at Penn State that I grappled with the spiritual ramifications of this frightening foundation.

Whether for home or away games, Joe always provided, for those players who wanted them, both Catholic and Protestant services, usually offered by the same two men. Since I was baptized in the Anglican Church of England, a Protestant denomination, I was accustomed to Protestant services. So, the first time I likely became acquainted with Reverend Tim McGill was during his Protestant service on Wednesday, August 28, 1991, in the Marriott Meadowlands (now the Renaissance Meadowlands), a few hours before the 9 p.m. start of the 1991 college football season, our game against the defending co-national champions, Georgia Tech, in the Kickoff Classic at Giants Stadium. During my junior year at the University Park campus, after careful reflection and many late Sunday-morning meetings with Rev. Tim (we called him "Brother Tim") over two years, I decided to walk my own path as an atheist. I've never looked back with an ounce of regret nor doubt.

As our unofficial team chaplain, you could say that it was Brother Tim's duty to help me. However, he wasn't bound by duty to Penn State, its football program, or Joe. Rev. Tim sat with me regularly for two years because that was his charge as a man devoted to the teachings of Jesus Christ in the New Testament. I was in an inner crisis. My family in New York was falling apart because my mother chose to deal with her cancer without the support of my father, sister, and me, plus I was losing my foothold as a starting receiver. My conversations with Brother Tim during that monumental time in my life were a welcome reprieve from it all. Those talks created links for me between my Bible study (growing up in convent school in England, Sunday school in Saint George's Church in Hempstead, Long Island, New York, and with Brother Tim), the comparative literature courses I took as an English major, and the African American Studies coursework I took. I was figuring out how to walk my life path comfortably in my own skin—physically, spiritually, and emotionally. The decision I made to seek Brother Tim's support during this crucial time in my life continues to serve me well. I learned to listen to and trust my inner voice, something I practiced throughout the process of writing this memoir.

Brother Tim gave me something I still carry. I wasn't a God-fearing young man, but I was patient, imperfect, and relentlessly hopeful—and I used the word "love" often, meaning it every time. Our talks more than thirty years ago stamped into my life what mentorship looks like and feels like. That gift never faded.

Professors Who Changed My Life's Course

I HAD SO MANY MEMORABLE PROFESSORS DURING MY undergraduate years at Penn State. Three stand out the most: Dr. LaVerne Gyant, Dr. Bernard Bell, and Dr. Richard Gibson.

Dr. LaVerne Gyant was the first teacher I had who inspired me to study African and African American history more deeply. I took with her what was called at the time Black Studies 100 during the fall semester of 1992, the start of my sophomore year. I've never been the same. She was an extremely passionate instructor with more than a little bit of an edge. I often wondered how my "white" peers took in her intensity, which could easily have been misunderstood as anger directed at them.

Now that I have been teaching similar content for a few decades, I understand, much more precisely, her classroom persona. Mine is similar, particularly in my African American literature course. The intensity was a visceral response to having to teach information that has always been marginalized, even though it should be normalized. It's maddening to teach students, year after year, who have never heard of "Scientific" or "Mitochondrial Eve," a woman who is the ancestor of all humans living today. She lived in Africa at least 200,000 years ago. Or that there is no such thing as a "white" race or a "black" race. We are one species, homo sapiens, 99.9 percent genetically similar. That 0.1 percent difference in our DNA accounts for all our physical differences, differences that have, too often, been turned into cavernous divides too many of us have neither the knowledge nor willpower to bridge. Dr. Gyant's teachings, as well as her willingness to mentor me outside our Penn State classroom, kept me firmly on the road to becoming a teacher conscious of my place in the capitalist structure as a man with brown skin, educated at one of the world's top universities.

I took Dr. Bell's course, "English 139–Black American Literature," during the spring semester of 1992. It was my first spring semester, and after that amazingly enjoyable Fiesta Bowl trip, where we destroyed the University of Tennessee. I'll never forget Dr. Bell because he gave me the first and only "F" I ever earned in college for an English paper. At the time, I was shocked.

Since sixth grade, I have been identified as an advanced reader and student. I never really studied exceptionally hard in school. I just stayed attentive, paid attention, and took good notes. For me, good note-taking was 90 percent of the studying. In high school, this enabled me to score a 1100 on the SAT in tenth grade, with no prep course, no studying. One of my twelfth-grade football teammates (I earned four varsity letters during my sophomore year) told me that he wished he had known sooner that he could have taken the SAT test as many times as desired. This was why I sat for the exam as a tenth-grader. I figured, why take the practice SAT test when I can take the real thing and see how well I do? I never had to retake it, since back then, you only needed a 700 to get a sports scholarship, and the offers started pouring in during the spring semester of my junior year. I graduated in the top 15 percent of my class, forty-seventh out of 370. I was the first News 12 Long Island Scholar Athlete Award winner in Uniondale High School history. I was a pretty confident student, even though I never studied hard enough to be on the honor roll. But then came Dr. Bell's "F." You could say that the bell finally tolled for me.

Seeing that "F" circled thickly at the top of my paper steamed my collar with shame. My English classes were always my favorite. There I was in the middle of central Pennsylvania, one of the few kids with brown skin attending Penn State, taking a class with one of the very few African American male professors, an esteemed English professor at that, and I forced him to give me a failing grade for my first paper.

To this day, I am extremely proud of my younger self for what I did next. I made an appointment to see Dr. Bell during his office hours so I could find out exactly what I needed to do to improve. For the better part of an hour, Dr. Bell savagely undressed me for having the audacity, the temerity, to hand into *him* a paper of such poor quality regarding subject matter (review the title of the course if you have forgotten) of substantial concern to our past, present, and future. He spent no time discussing my content, structure, and logic. He just spent the time firmly and succinctly attacking my pride. Here's a fair summation of that first meeting:

"Mr. Williams, do you think because you look like me, I'm going to let you waltz through this course giving me a level of effort and thought that pales in comparison to your white peers?"

"I do not, sir."

"Then why on earth would you submit to me a paper of such low quality?"

Silence.

"Are you aware that you are no longer in high school?"

"I am now, sir."

"We will see, Mr. Williams. If you submit to me another low-caliber paper, you will absolutely not pass this course, do you understand me?"

"Yes, sir. Thank you for your time, sir."

I poured myself into that next paper. I've never been so proud of earning a "C" for a course in my life. That verbal beatdown from Dr.

Bell taught me a lot. I needed and deserved it. I didn't leave that meeting or his course feeling shamed, abused, or insulted. Quite the opposite. Dr. Bell recognized exactly how to motivate me. I took his course because he was a man with brown skin who was a scholar of the English language, something we as Black men are never mistaken for. I sat in class, mesmerized by his erudition and articulation, not to mention his turtlenecks worn with a blazer and slacks. His clean, bald head also impressed me.

It was a long while before I became conscious of how deeply Dr. Bell's classroom persona affected me. By the end of my sophomore year, I had shaved my head bald. For the first ten years of my teaching career, I wore suits to work. Today, I teach an African American literature course for seniors at Uniondale High School. When needed, I do not hesitate to let my students know how much I love and respect them by telling them the unadulterated truth in a way that connects with them logically, psychologically, emotionally, and culturally. I chose to be a teacher, in part, to be Dr. Bell for other students. That outstanding man left me no choice but to up my game.

I remain grateful to Dr. Bell.

Of all my undergrad professors, I spent the most time with Dr. Richard Gibson. Richard was the first person who took me to a gun range and showed me how to shoot handguns. For a year, we met regularly for dinner at Golden Wok, a Chinese restaurant that used to be on the corner of College Avenue and South Atherton Street. Richard's apartment was a block away on College Ave, and that restaurant was one of my favorite places to eat, so meeting there was a no-brainer.

He and I spent many hours talking about our lives, who we were, and who we were trying to be. We also talked a lot about history, politics, and education. He and I were kindred spirits, people who very much marched to our own beat, come hell or high water. He was involved in the civil rights movement and unionization (and where those two movements intersected) beginning in Detroit, Michigan, where he grew up. For most of his life, he had a deep affection for social justice actions and movements, and lived that life on the front lines. While my other most favored professors were Henry Louis Gates Jr., Cornel West, and Angela Davis, Richard was more like John Brown.

Richard told me I was the best student teacher he had ever seen. That gave me confidence that I was pursuing the right profession and on track to be what I wanted to be: someone who makes an impact. About thirty years later, as I sit with only a few years left before I retire, becoming an English teacher was one of the smartest decisions I've ever made. I love going to work every day and being with my students, who are Uniondale kids, like me. I love them and give them my best every day.

The time Richard invested in me mattered. He impacted countless lives, and mine was among them.

Sandy Meyer was an academic counselor for athletics with whom I became very close. Here we were catching up in the football letterman's lounge, fall 2025.

Starter No More

I WASN'T AS FOCUSED ON BEING THE BEST FOOTBALL PLAYER I could be after my second year at Penn State. Unbeknownst to us, my mother was dying from malignant tumors that ravaged her body. My dad and sister knew she wasn't well, but they didn't realize the full extent of the issue. Mom kept her illness a secret, a decision from which we never recovered as a family.

During the '93 season, I received reports from my sister and father about how poorly my mom was doing. When I spoke with her, I said I wanted to leave school to be with her. She'd have none of that. That was the season I began playing soft, the season Joe and Kenny Jackson, our receivers coach, kept me as a starter as long as possible, hoping I would work through whatever it was I was going through. I felt, then and now, that they gave me every benefit of the doubt. But finally, my poor, uninspired play forced them to demote me.

I've rarely thought a lot about the role Fran Ganter, Joe's long-time offensive coordinator and running backs coach, played in me not playing even more than I did. It was much easier pointing fingers at others than at myself, but it's usually much more productive dealing with the changes I ought to make in myself to improve my circumstances. I needed to handle my family in Uniondale better, coming undone because of my mother's illness (cancer) and eventual death, but I couldn't.

However, I was never convinced that Frannie, as Joe and a lot of us called him, liked me that much. First, I was a receiver, and Fran always gave preferential treatment to the running backs whenever and wherever possible. I never had the chance to be one of the deep kickoff return guys. Even though I was the fastest guy on the team, we almost never got really good kickoff returns, and we never ran one back for a touchdown. I was always pissed that we only had running backs in those positions. Fran was the coach who made this decision. I should have had a shot to prove myself.

Second, I didn't get to play in the '94 Rose Bowl because of Fran Ganter. He apologized to me after the game for not thinking of putting me in at the end. I didn't care at all about his apology, and I was baffled that he offered it. At the time, and for many years after, I was genuinely pissed that I stood there beside him on the sideline, watching others get some time on the field during that historic game. But large parts of me also felt that I truly did not deserve to play in that game. I wanted to be in a seat in the stadium sitting next to mom, who made the trip out by herself to soak in the moment, knowing her son was a part of the spectacle of it all, though riding the bench, as was the case during the season.

I couldn't have felt more disconnected from what was happening on that field that day, or that awesome season. I was late to a meeting with Kenny Jackson and the receivers during the days leading up to the game because I was with my mom. I knew she wasn't doing well, and I didn't care about being on time for that meeting. Fifteen months later, she would be dead. But I never told anyone she was sick. Even I didn't know just how badly she was doing.

The third reason I felt Coach Ganter didn't care that much about me? I think he thought I was too much of an intellectual to deserve significant playing time, an affliction suffered by many football coaches. There is a lengthy list of great football players who have played at Penn State, at many other great universities, as well as in the NFL, who had brains galore. Football coaches always say they want smart, tough, disciplined players. Too many (not all) of these coaches want players who are *football* smart, but not smart enough to be a university dean or president. This is ironic, given Joe's "Grand Experiment." It was Joe's experiment, not Frannie's.

As we were coming off the elevator and heading to the pregame meal at Iowa in '93, Coach Ganter got on my elbow and said to me, "Justin, I can see you being a dean or president at a university someday." After a few steps, we both went different directions to find our tables. The comment caught me off guard so much that I couldn't respond. It has been seared into my consciousness for over three decades and counting.

Under normal circumstances, it would have been a charming thing to say to a young man. The problem was that moment was the only time Fran Ganter looked in my direction to utter a complete thought that had nothing to do with football while I was a member of the Penn State football team. He and I never spoke about anything at all having to do with me as a person. Not a single word. I had no idea what he knew about me that would make him say that to me. All I had to evaluate the origin of that comment was Fran's general indifference towards me when he wasn't giving me a play to run into our quarterback. Otherwise, I never noticed him looking at me unless it was in a way that made me feel like an outsider to his plans.

On the sideline during games, even when I was playing a lot, I always felt that he'd prefer to be sending someone else in to convey the play to our quarterback. You can just tell when someone is feeling you and when they are not. Fran never seemed to like me that much. So, my twenty-year-old self didn't hear a compliment. What I heard Frannie say was, "I don't really think you need football as much as your teammates. You clearly have a future beyond football. You don't need the NFL like some of these other guys."

In sports, as well as in the game of life, sometimes, things work against you. My inability to focus on the practice field made it very easy for him to cast me aside. Probably, if Joe didn't like me so much, I would have been demoted even sooner. I know I didn't deserve to be the starter any longer, looking back. Later that day, in Iowa, I would lose my position as a starter forever.

I remember the exact moment. We were at a sold-out Kinnick Stadium, a big game for me personally because two of my mentors—one of my high school football coaches, Phil Coppola, and his cousin, Mike Ninivaggi—flew out to the game from Long Island. *Long Island Newsday* did a feature story during the week leading up to the game. Seven players from Long Island played in that game, four for Penn State.

On the field with my high school teammate Fritz Fequiere at the University of Iowa, fall 1993. Photo credit: Phil Coppola

My high school teammate, Gerald "Fritz" Fequiere, was the starting right guard for the Iowa offense and a member of its 500-pound bench-press club. My junior year playing football for the Uniondale Football Knights was Gerald's senior season. He starred at right offensive tackle and defensive tackle while I was in my first year starting at quarterback and second year starting at free safety. That season, we had the highest scoring offense on Long Island and made the playoffs for the first time in school history. We bowed out of the playoffs in the first round, mainly due to significant injuries to key teammates in the final game of the regular season. We have mostly fond memories of that season, though. Our offensive line averaged six foot three, 260 pounds. Gerald was six foot four, 270. He had a stellar season.

So much so that his game film was reviewed by many college football recruiters. This was incredibly fortunate for me, because I featured all over his highlight reel, especially at quarterback. Gerald was a major reason I started receiving full scholarship offers in the spring semester of my junior year, soon after he signed his letter of intent to attend Iowa. One of the reasons Gerald chose Iowa was that the black-and-gold uniforms were almost identical to our high school's black-and-gold uniforms. In college, we found ourselves playing on the same Saturday, on the same field, each wearing two iconic collegiate football uniforms.

After the game, Mike and Phil jumped out of the stands behind the Penn State bench and took a picture of us. I love the picture. It represents a lot of hard work put in by two kids from Uniondale, as well as the families and educators who poured enough into us for us to stand together at that moment in the history of our lives, the zenith of our powers as young men with skills enough to be serious contributors on teams coached by legends of the sport, Hayden Fry and Joe Paterno. That picture also captures the last game I remember being a serious factor in our wide receiver starting rotation.

The last ball I ever had thrown my way at Penn State occurred just before halftime. The name of the play in the huddle was "Robert 56 Lion." We ran this play multiple times that day on our way to a 31–0 victory. "Robert" represented the formation, with two receivers to the right side of the offensive formation: me in the slot as our "X" or flanker receiver, and Bobby Engram as our "Z" or split end receiver. Kyle Brady was on the opposite side of this formation in a three-point stance (one hand on the ground) in a traditional tight end position we called the "Y." Kerry Collins was our QB under center. He did not start the game but was brought in during the first half to replace a struggling John Sacca. Behind him were Ki-Jana Carter at tailback and Jon Witman at fullback. The number five stood for "50 protection," which represented to the offensive lineman and the running backs how many of them were responsible for protecting Kerry from being sacked, while also letting us all know that Kerry was taking five big steps backward, planting, and looking to deliver the ball to an open receiver. There would be no run play fake (play-action) with this protection. The number six let all the receivers know which pass routes to run, along with the "Lion designation."

My job was to come off the line slowly to let Kyle move across the defense in my direction, as I moved across towards him, but shallower. We were essentially crisscrossing each other, me at about seven yards, him at twelve yards. Kerry's job was to read the linebackers to see which one of us would pop open then hit us in stride during our crossing routes.

I remember feeling like I was wide open as I came across the field, now even with Bucky Greeley, our center, who had snapped the ball to Kerry. Iowa, as anticipated, was in a zone coverage. I think it was first down, ten yards to go. We were in two-minute offense mode, trying to score before the end of the first half.

I had started the play off the ball, about twelve yards to Bucky's right. By the time I got even with him, or just past him, I looked for Kerry but couldn't see him very well through the raw tonnage of humanity in front of him, some of them protecting him in blue and white, others trying to sack him in black and gold. He couldn't have seen me clearly for very long, but long enough to know I was open. The ball came my way. Because of the congestion, I didn't pick up the ball out of his hand. By the time it got to me, it was a bit behind my left ear, opposite the direction I was running. Reacting too late, the ball went through my hands and fell to the ground behind me, incomplete. As I jogged off the field, it was clear that Kenny Jackson and Fran Ganter expected me to catch that ball. It's likely others in the same situation would have been given some grace. Whatever meager grace I had ran out with that play, an accumulation of weeks of uninspired play after starting the season on the injured reserve list with a thigh contusion suffered during preseason two-a-day practices.

For the rest of my time as a player at Penn State, I remember little about the games because I only got on the field during garbage time or special teams. I returned to practicing hard with focus and discipline but never got another chance to be a starter. Although I earned three varsity letters in football and one for indoor track, I did not play enough during the legendary 1994 season to earn a letter. For a very long time, I felt shame and embarrassment at that fact. It took the better part of thirty years to feel okay within myself to even write it.

Why? Why did it take me so long to get over not lettering in '94? Pride is probably the most succinct, honest answer I can give, even though one of the biggest takeaways from my college football experience is "pride is your most useless asset." My mom gave me ten laminated life lessons when she, my dad, my sister, and my godmother, Peggy Cook, from England, dropped me off to begin college. I kept them with me throughout my time at Penn State. Today, as a fifty-two-year-old man, this one, about pride, is the only one I remember. It's the one lesson that took me the longest to fully understand.

An Ambivalent Leader

Every day I stepped into our football facility was a day I wished I weren't there. I wanted to be home. Kenny and Joe were right; I wasn't tough enough. I wasn't tough enough to put my mother's condition out of my mind enough so that when I stepped across that blue line painted around the practice field, I focused on being the best football player I could be every day. I felt confused and scared about what was happening back in Long Island. I couldn't let it go.

I recall seeing an immortalized quote from the Penn State great Mike Reid around our facilities during my freshman year: "There's a thousand reasons for failure—and not a single excuse." It's one of the various expressions I came across at Penn State that have never left my consciousness since my undergraduate days. I was keenly aware of that truth—one I still believe today—as I struggled to do my job because my focus was scattered and my mind wasn't clear.

The most important lesson I learned as an undergraduate football player in Happy Valley was this: You have to handle your business. No matter how heavy your personal life feels, the people in charge have time for only one thing—how well you do your job. It was a hard lesson, and I learned it later than I should have. Too late to end up on the cover of *Sports Illustrated* like the exceptional player who replaced me, Freddie Scott—but early enough to build a good life.

A Season of Indoor Track

During the spring semester of 1994, College Football Hall of Fame inductee (December 8, 2026), Ki-Jana Carter and I decided to run track for Coach Harry Groves. We went together to meet with him towards the end of the fall '93 semester and received Coach Paterno's blessing after we returned from the Florida Citrus Bowl in January. During our meeting with Coach Groves, we discussed our high school track experiences and what our college track practices and meet schedules would be like.

There was a stark difference between being a full-scholarship football player at Penn State and being a member of the men's track team. We didn't fly anywhere. We took coach buses to our meets, whether it was to Ann Arbor, Michigan (site of the Big Ten Championship indoor meet that season), Syracuse, New York, or the University of Virginia. The entourage of people traveling to meets was also smaller. Road trips were filled with card games, banter about anything and everything, and mall shopping. I loved buying fitted hats from the schools we played at and wearing them around campus or to parties. I couldn't buy that gear downtown or at the Nittany Mall—it marked where I'd been. Travel became its own kind of classroom. Being a scholarship athlete let me see parts of the country I'd never imagined, and experiencing those places through two different sports only deepened the lesson.

I spent quality time getting to know Ki-Jana even better than I already knew him. All I ever wanted to do around Ki was laugh. His laughter had a way of pulling you in and lifting the room. There was no way around it. I shake my head when I think about how much fun I always had and still have anytime I'm with him.

Track was a welcome reprieve before the start of summer workouts that prepared our football teammates and us for one of the greatest football seasons in not only Penn State history, but in the history of the Big Ten and college football, in general. Expectations within the football program spring '94 were through the roof. We knew we were going to be good that fall, not having another collapse like the one we had in '92. Of that, we were certain.

As much as Joe and our football coaches would have preferred that we play spring ball, Joe didn't put up any resistance to us running track, so no one else could stop us. Everyone knew Ki and I were probably the two fastest guys on the team. We could run all day, and, by then, we had played in a lot of big games. As it turned out, my football time as a star was over while Ki's was about to hit legendary status. However, at that time, the only thing that was assured was that we were going to have an excellent time running track. We never talked about competing against each other in a race, but it happened one Saturday afternoon at the Greenberg Sports Complex, at home, steps from where we lived in Nittany Apartments.

The place was as packed as that facility could be without anyone getting injured. It was nowhere as lovely as the indoor track arena they have now, and it was the poorest of any facility we ran in that season. My mom took a bus from Long Island to get to the meet that day, as she didn't like to drive long distances. At some point, word got out that Ki and I were going to race in the 55-meter dash, a rare distance to run in college back then, as compared to the 60-meter dash. Today, you generally don't see anyone at that level running that distance anymore. Regardless, there was a buzz in the air. Who would win? I felt like the expectation was that Ki would be triumphant. He was a stud Penn State running back with crazy breakaway speed. Nothing in that statement conveys the slightest bit of hyperbole. He was 215 pounds of fast-twitch explosiveness. I was a 185-pound receiver.

I won my semifinal heat, and so did he. In today's social media and cell phone world, an even bigger mob of people would have surged across campus to get to that sports complex before the showdown. But by the standards of the day, the crowd was enough. I felt like the underdog, but I was also confident. I had had a pretty serious track career at Uniondale High School, one of the best track programs in the eastern United States during the eighties for sure. Our 4 x 400-meter relay squad won the Championship of America final against the best teams in America and the Caribbean at the Penn Relays a decade earlier. I competed at the Penn Relays multiple times, as well as multiple county, Long Island, and state championship meets. I was a bit of a track fanatic, truth be told. I followed the sport closely, still do.

Standing in front of my starting blocks before our first and only encounter on a track, I was in lane five while Ki was to my left in lane three. One person crouched between us, and all eight lanes were occupied with a sprinter trying to win this race. I felt there was only one person on that track who could give me a run for my money in the 55-meter sprint: the dude who was a few months away from sprinting a similar distance on our very first offensive play in the January 1995 Rose Bowl in Pasadena, leaving behind the entire Oregon defense in a sprint that will live forever in Penn State and Rose Bowl lore.

BOOM! The gun released us from the blocks. I got off great, as I so often did. By thirty meters, I couldn't feel anyone on me and couldn't see anyone in my peripheral vision. I held on for a comfortable win. I remember our football teammate, Tisen Thomas, and our track teammate, James Robbins, at the finish line, looking impressed.

Tisen snapped a picture of us crossing the finish line, me ahead, my right hand up with a number one sign. He gave me that photo, but it has disappeared into the ether. I remember someone telling me they had clocked me with a handheld stopwatch in 6.12 seconds. I won the 200-meter dash later that day as well.

I was really glad Mom got to see me compete that day; she was two years from dying. She hated watching me play football; it made her too nervous, she said. The main reason she made the trip alone was that my father and I were not on speaking terms, dumb father-son stuff. He and I barely spoke my last two years competing at PSU, which added to my inability to really enjoy the 1993–95 seasons, partly why I don't remember much about those seasons. Losing my starting position to Freddie Scott during the fall '93 season was an inevitable part of my steadily collapsing life, culminating in my mom's death on March 9, 1996.

So, winning those two races that day, one against a PSU legend who is the most down-to-earth brother you'll ever meet, was huge. I worked hard to avoid the pain I felt about my mom traveling all that way by bus, just to see me run two races, then get back on the bus to immediately return home. I have since understood that although she wouldn't or couldn't tell me, she knew she was going to die soon. She flew out to California to the Rose Bowl a few months later.

Mom hung out with Barbara Woolridge, a woman many PSU football players knew most affectionately, until her passing, as "The Cookie Lady." If she adopted you, you gained the privilege of being part of her "Cookie Crew." She delivered a very large bag of homemade chocolate chip cookies to our door at Nittany Apartments, along with a typed letter full of bits and pieces about her life and her thoughts on the season, Joe, and the team. Along the way, she named me president of the Cookie Crew. She picked me up and took me out for dinner every so often. That woman loved Penn State football. We loved her. I loved her tons. I miss her. I miss my mom.

As you get older, living gets harder and harder, in part because of all the emotional scars that never fully heal when you lose people you love.

On average, Joe convinced a very high percentage of relatively well-polished young male high school graduates (whether from single- or two-parent households) to attend Penn State and the football program he held sway over. What do I mean by well-polished? This book, in summary, aims to paint a picture of precisely that, as it pertains to a great many of my Penn State football brothers and me. But to be succinct, it means the majority of young men who played in Joe's program came from homes that provided enough emotional stability and financial security to afford these boys enough opportunities to read and write enough words to do well enough in school to gain academic entrance into a university like The Pennsylvania State University.

One of the biggest reasons Penn State was a no-brainer for me was that the program graduated a higher percentage of its full-scholarship players year in and year out than just about every top football program in the country. Joe's football program consistently produced a higher percentage of African American players who graduated than any other powerhouse program in the country.

My experience at Penn State shaped me in many ways. The racial dynamics of being a full grant-in-aid athlete at one of the largest universities in our country is, for many of us, an interesting cultural two-step that very much prepares you to grapple with similar issues to come throughout your adult life.

During my undergraduate years, I heavily identified with being a football player, a brown-skinned man (I'm not Black; the words on this page are black, like my eyebrows), a New Yorker, and a British West Indian. Similar to many other campuses across the land, football players are the big dogs among the student body.

When I arrived at Penn State's gorgeous University Park campus in State College, Pennsylvania, as a full scholarship award winner in Joe Paterno's famed NCAA football program, the university had no affiliation with an athletic conference. During my first two years as a Nittany Lion, we were a football independent.

It wasn't until the football program joined the Big Ten Conference in 1993 that I fully understood some of the perks of being athletically independent. As an independent team, we had our own cafeteria for breakfast and dinner every day. We lost breakfast among ourselves once we entered the Big Ten. Each senior player was allowed to receive a car rental during bowl games when we were independent. This opportunity was lost as members of the Big Ten.

Ironically, now that players are being paid for their talent and skills directly by Penn State, all the benefits we had as an independent have returned in spades. Football players at PSU were always, by far, the leading revenue earner in PSU athletics (https://www.si.com/college/pennstate/football/what-it-costs-to-run-the-penn-state-football-team-01jjw9qtvt9p). As of this writing, there are only seven universities in the country whose athletic program turns a profit. Penn State is one of them, and it has been one of them for a very long time (excluding the COVID-19 years), thanks to a powerhouse football program made famous by Joe Paterno.

However, what is rarely discussed among college sports fans are the advantages that come to universities, outside of sports, with being a member of a conference like the Big Ten. I recall Joe telling us that we would have access to every library of every university in the conference. The Big Ten Academic Alliance, formed in 1958, also benefits professors, who are supported in collaborating on research and projects with their conference peers. I very much remember these things seeming to be as important to Joe as any advantages we gained athletically. I loved that about him.

I finished my undergraduate coursework in English education with an African American Studies minor in December of 1995. I was in attendance for the first two official functions at the Bryce Jordan Center, a PSU men's basketball game and graduation in January of 1996. Like many young men at such a moment in life, I was feeling very uncertain about where my life was heading. The biggest question looming was whether I was going to take a shot at the National Football League or get into teaching and coaching. The question was to be addressed of course, but not in the way I thought. Life often has its own way of instilling lessons. And our greatest lessons are often the most painful.

In the locker room after the Outback Bowl on January 1, 1996, we were all wet. We had just defeated Auburn University at Raymond James Stadium in Tampa, Florida. Six inches of rain fell in that stadium that day, prompting some media to aptly rename that inaugural bowl sponsorship for the Outback food chain the "Mud Bowl." It was great to end my career victorious, but in my head, I wasn't much of a winner.

I was a special team's player, someone whose time had come and gone to be on the first team. I remained pissed at myself for becoming resigned to being a backup and perennial special teamer. I hadn't felt like I had any fight in me since the '93 season when I officially lost my starting position to Freddie Scott, who, like a supremely high percentage of guys with whom I played, was and is a phenomenal man.

As I took off my uniform for the final time, I felt relieved—relieved I no longer had to look into the face of my position coach, Kenny Jackson, and see disappointment mixed with disgust. Or was it indifference? It became clear to me that Kenny's mind had been made up during the '93 season that I wasn't good enough to start in front of Freddie. As long as Freddie did what he had to do (which he did very well), I would never sniff the field when it mattered. Kenny was correct for feeling this way, but he never knew the real reason why.

Fourth Quarter

The Choice

I met Joseph V. Paterno for the first time in June 1990 on the University Park campus while attending a three-day, two-night football camp for high school athletes (I don't think any college does camps this long anymore!). I was being recruited by assistant coach Joe "Buddy" Sarra. Staying in one of the East Halls dorms, Buddy told me he wanted me to meet Joe in between one of the four (!) practice sessions we held per day, just after lunch. Buddy explained that I would have to run there, following him in his car, because it was against NCAA rules for him to drive me to the office of the head coach.

Joe was in his sixties back then, taller than I thought he would be. He didn't have a single gray hair on his head. He wore a coat, tie, and nice slacks, as was always the case whenever I saw him around the office. Professional. The practice field was the only place you'd ever see Joe in a sweater or windbreaker, always in comfortable khaki or blue slacks. Not that he wouldn't frequently make the knot in the simple-knotted tie looser or have his sleeves rolled up with his jacket off. But you'd never see him in a Penn State T-shirt and shorts or sweatpants.

You had a better chance of seeing Bobby Bowden decked out in clothes with "Florida State" written all over them in big, clearly visible letters than you did seeing Joe dressing like that. Joe preferred understatement; if you accept it, it is fair to say that dressing in a suit is an understatement. But coach wore suits and colors that were not at all flashy. I don't know who rubbed off on who, Penn State on him or vice-versa, but I know what most of us would bet.

I was also initially taken aback at how gently Joe spoke. I've witnessed countless times since this first meeting that when he walked into a room and started talking, a stillness fell over everyone within earshot. Part of this, of course, was because he was a legend. The other part? If you move around too much, you won't be able to catch a darn word he said—unless he was angry. I figure only a handful of people have ever heard the man speak when he's truly angry, aside from his wife, Sue, his children, and anyone who ever played for him.

My first meeting with Joe didn't last more than five minutes. I didn't fully understand why Buddy brought me in to meet him. I assumed lots of other guys were going to get the chance to meet him, too. There were around six hundred high school athletes representing, largely, Pennsylvania, New Jersey, and New York. To that point, I knew they were interested in me, but even during that meeting, Joe never stated anything to me like, "You ought to be a Penn Stater" or "I'm really interested in having you play for us." I certainly would remember if he did. I left that meeting feeling impressed and flattered. I wonder how many thousands of people have felt similarly upon encountering that icon.

The understated nature of my developing relationship with Coach Paterno continued during the summer of 1990, when he mailed four handwritten letters to my Long Island home. In one of them, he wrote, "I've never coached anyone from England before." He never, in any of them, came any closer than that to informing me that he wanted me to play for The Pennsylvania State University, and I wasn't a hundred percent sure until Buddy told me over the phone that they wouldn't mind if I gave a verbal commitment to attend. I loved this understated approach. It appealed to my sensibilities.

Like the majority of men who played at Penn State, many universities all over the country contacted me either by phone or letter, directly or indirectly, expressing their interest in my athletic prowess. I didn't have to go to study in State College, but I verbally committed to attend school there just before the start of my high school senior year because I felt comfortable there in every single way I needed to feel cozy. Also, like most guys who have played for him, the head football coach is a very significant reason.

After the 1992 season, our final as an athletically independent football program and one that left an extremely bitter taste in the mouths of everyone associated with the team, Joe systematically continued laying the foundation for what would become the elegantly successful 1994 season. During the '92 season and through spring drills in '93, I learned everything I'll ever need to know about Joe Paterno. I also learned the essence of what needs to be known regarding how to lead a dynamic organization away from disaster's brink and back in the direction of greatness.

Joe was an enormously talented, knowledgeable, and principled man and coach. Unfortunately, he may very well have excelled long enough to become a victim of his own successes and abilities. The Penn State football program, like any entity that has existed for some time, has gone through periods of prosperity and struggle. But by broadening our gaze, weaknesses in the organization he brought to national prominence can be seen.

My Appointment

During our first squad meeting after returning from getting stomped by Stanford at the Blockbuster Bowl in January of 1993, Joe said that any player who wanted to see him to discuss their thoughts about the program should make an appointment ASAP. After a few days of deliberation, I decided to take him at his word, even though I was only a redshirt freshman. On the morning of our appointment, I put on one of my suits and a tie, gathered the notes I had made regarding what I wished to say, and headed to the office. Of course, I was fifteen minutes early.

I was sweaty-palm nervous. I hadn't yet reached a point where I could refer to Joe, either to his face or in my head, by his first name. Our meeting was the first time that I would be alone with him. Voices in my subconscious continued to try to talk me out of what I was about to do, even as he welcomed me into his office and offered me a seat. I calmed myself down, believing firmly that Coach wanted to hear what I had to say.

He didn't sit behind his desk, but next to me in identical chairs, so we faced each other, Joe no more than five feet away from me. He had on, as usual, slacks, shirt and tie. I took out the paper with my notes and began my thoroughly rehearsed presentation on what I thought went wrong during the 1992 season and how we could improve going forward. My thoughts weren't written word-for-word, but were just keywords or phrases to which I could glance. Many thanks to my Speech Communication 100 professor, from whom I learned a lot the previous spring.

Coach Paterno never interrupted and didn't speak—not once—until I was finished. He just listened with one side of his mouth curled slightly upward as I went through my four or five points. His demeanor was soothing, but I was still a bit pensive about how receptive he'd be to my critiques of our program. However, it was OUR program, and I wanted to win. To this day, I cannot stand being a part of an organization I perceive to be ineffective, inefficient and/or fomenting a culture of disharmony, selfishness, or lack of courage. It's vital to me to help make things better or I have to leave. I didn't know that about myself when I was nineteen years old, but this meeting was an early manifestation.

We were not performing optimally as a football program. Things needed to change. I had strong pride in our program and thoughts on some cures. I absolutely had to share. To do otherwise was not who I was, not who I am.

I remember two of the points I shared. One regarded the use of different colored jerseys during practice, which represented first, whether you played offense or defense, and second, where you were on the depth chart. I thought we needed to get rid of the system because there were too many instances where guys wearing backup jerseys were either playing more than the starter or perceived to be (by the players) better than the guy wearing the first team blue jersey. It was my feeling that too many players believed the system didn't represent what it was supposed to represent.

The other point I made was that we were far too predictable on offense that year. That season, if I didn't start the game, I came in on the second play. Most of the time, Tisen Thomas, Chip LaBarca, or I ran in the plays given to us by offensive coordinator Fran Ganter.

Early in the season, I led the team in yards per catch, but I finished the season with seven catches for 179 yards and one touchdown. Too many times, O. J. McDuffie, the split or "Z" receiver, or Richie Anderson, our tailback, were the go-to options. Stanford University, under four-time Super Bowl-winning coach Bill Walsh, exploited this tendency to perfection, double-teaming O. J. and/or putting eight men within five yards of the line of scrimmage to contain our vaunted running game. My position, the "X" receiver, was left one-on-one with the Stanford cornerback. I wanted to scream every time I came off the field during the game, but doing so wasn't part of my character at that point. I felt that if I or anyone else was out there between the white lines as a receiver with O. J., we should be a threat. Otherwise, don't have us out there.

When I was finished, the first thing Joe said was, "You want a coaching job?"

I don't remember anything he said after that because I was so relieved he was receptive. The color system employed during practice remained for the rest of my stay in the program, though it disappeared sometime after I graduated (not because of my advice years before, I'm sure). The offense became a bit less predictable, though I'm certainly not the sole reason. In fact, the '93 season was the first time in Penn State football history that we used a four-receiver offensive package. I remain grateful that I played for a coach of Joe's stature who never felt too big to leave himself open to taking suggestions, if not critique, from his players, particularly those as young as I was then. You could always make an appointment to speak with him. He always said so. And it was true. He wasn't too big where giving his players his time was out of bounds. This is part of why I feel he is legendary.

The Joe I Know

I WATCHED JOE VERY CLOSELY DURING THE 1992 SEASON, MUCH more closely than I did in '91. The difference was that I redshirted my freshman year but traveled and dressed for every game. At that time, I didn't fully realize how close I was to playing. However, because I didn't play in any games, I didn't have as good a feel for Joe's explanations to the media regarding our play. On top of that, we won almost all our games in 1991, so my ole ball coach didn't have too many difficult press conferences. Nineteen ninety-two was, for me, shockingly different.

Joe took it on the chin plenty from the media that year. Too many of those press conferences were difficult for me to watch. I felt embarrassed for Joe. We're Penn State. And we almost lost to the University of Cincinnati in our opening game! We had beaten them 81–0 the year before, trying hard not to score during the second half. We rattled off five straight wins to start the season, then lost to the University of Miami, followed by a let-down loss to a sharp, tough Boston College team coached by eventual two-time Super Bowl champion Tom Coughlin.

We lost five of our last seven games, a stretch of football unheard of at that time by a Paterno-coached team that had not suffered monumental injury. After the previous year's ending rank of #2 in the nation, we were supposed to be on the upswing, a serious contender for a national championship. If the nation didn't feel that way, we certainly did. But we were a sinking ship after the Miami loss. It showed all over Joe's face during that stretch.

I saw sweat on Joe's upper lip and brow many times while responding to tough questions about what was happening. Seeing those droplets of pride, disappointment, and tenacity were key in helping me to fully understand what a big deal it all was. I had the idea that Joe was impervious to everything. But everyone feels pressure at some point in life. Everyone. Joe taught me that. He also taught me that successful people handle pressure better than those who do not succeed quite as much. One big reason? Successful folks are not paralyzed by the thought of failure.

I got to learn, up close and personal in 1992, my second year in college when I was nineteen that Joe Paterno was a real guy who had a great many people to answer to, whether we won or lost, and that he was made of the stuff necessary to endure. A quite particular feeling came over me as I watched him get grilled that year, sitting in the hot seat. For me, the guy I saw being treated like some common football coach at Podunk State was the same person who sat in the den of the house in which I grew up, charming the heck out of my parents.

Joe was the guy to whom my parents entrusted with their only son, confident that Joe was serious about finishing what they had started. The way he carried himself, the way he spoke, and the things he had accomplished were the reasons it was a no-brainer to attend this exceptional program and our great school. He, as well as the caliber of guys he brought in to play next to me, was much of the reason I'd fight to stay on a block a little longer, to push a little harder, to dig a little deeper. I wanted to contribute to the continued justification of his "Grand Experiment." I wanted everyone to know the "experiment" was alive and thriving; still producing the sort of results to which Penn Staters everywhere could be proud. Joe was always watching, someway, somehow. But we failed him, failed ourselves by not living up to our expectations.

Those hard press conferences made me realize how many people outside the stadiums in which we played were watching. Back then, and coming out of high school, it was difficult to comprehend how many people cared about the Penn State football program. In that moment, Joe stepped down from his iconic pedestal and became flesh and blood to me, as I watched hostile fans curse at him and reporters press him with pointed questions about his age—questions that strongly suggested the game, and his feel for it, had passed him by. My coach sat there and faced the music. Always. I saw how hard it was for him. But a real adult always faces the music. My father taught me that. Being able to watch Joe from that unique vantage point made me much more aware of the downsides of fame. It also made me fiercely loyal to my coach.

Tough circumstances are the sledgehammer by which character is chiseled. Coach Paterno was an expert at creating an environment for his players at Penn State that was packed to the rafters with difficulties and love. The University Park campus was the anvil upon which we were pounded into fully mature men. You absolutely could not complete a degree in Joe's program without having aspects of the man engraved upon your consciousness. Joe pounded into us the value of being on time for everything, to eat breakfast, to keep our noses in the books, to remember that football was a high second but schoolwork was an undisputed first, to get the heck up when you hit the ground, fight like the devil but always keep our wits about us, have a little swagger but comport ourselves as a gentleman should, put in the work it takes to be something special, always being in the habit of remaining so, and BE ON TIME! It didn't end there.

Don Ferrell, our academic counselor, lovingly prodded us to remain diligent in our academic progress when he had to (and he had to A LOT with many guys), but much of the time, his presence was a calming influence. Dr. John Thomas, the superb strength and conditioning coach, directed the chiseling of our bodies and spirits during relentless and excruciatingly intense workouts that made all else we had to endure easy. Knowing you had to make the grade was an added burden we knew others around the country did not share nearly as often. Keeping yourself properly groomed at all times (e.g., no chin whiskers), fighting the desire to excessively celebrate—these were some of the things that separated us from the rest.

It was harder to win championships at Penn State for these reasons. It was harder to win when you're playing for a man with honor and firmly grounded principles for which there is no equivocation or no wiggle room. We were always aware that winning every game was harder for us, especially during the early nineties. The program, philosophically in terms of x's and o's, was in transition.

My first two years at Penn State, our final two years as a football independent, things remained business as usual: dominate games with a conservative offense focused on an intimidating running game and a fundamentally sound, physically talented, and aggressive defense. That philosophy remained good enough to beat our usual rivals from the east like Syracuse, Rutgers, and Pitt. However, year in and year out, that strategy wasn't getting the job done against the sport's superpowers.

Many offensive players during my first two years didn't like that, almost without fail, our game plans would become glaringly conservative in the prominent matchups on our schedule. USC in '91 and Miami in '91 and '92 are quality examples. As players, we wanted to be free to display our full talents during those games, especially when we knew all eyes would be on us. However, as the saying goes, youth is most often wasted on the young. Fortunately, our exuberance was tempered by a coaching staff with over a century of football experience. And those teams didn't exactly open the floodgates against us either. In big-time games between topflight teams, most of the time, a few plays are the difference in the ball game.

All in all, the best way I can summarize the Joe I know is by sharing the last private, formal meeting I had with him at the end of my fifth year, a week or two after my graduation in January of 1996. I needed to know whether it was worth going through the process of trying to latch on to a team in the National Football League.

As usual, I wore a jacket, slacks, and a tie to my private meeting with Joe, made by appointment. Regardless of how busy he was, I never had a problem scheduling with him, and he never canceled or made me feel rushed. In fact, I always felt like the most important thing in Joe's life when I sat in his office during the four meetings I had with him during my undergraduate years.

I walked in and said, "Thank you for your time, as always Joe," as I took my seat.

"Okay. What's on your mind?"

"What's your opinion about me playing professionally?"

"Well, I think you'd do fine. You can run, and you don't get hurt. You could be a pro as long as you'd want."

As he finished that last sentence, my mind was already racing ahead, planning when I would head to Pittsburgh to sign with an agent who had been courting me—and a few other players—since we returned to campus for the spring semester, once our college eligibility had run out. I mentally planned my workouts to be in optimal condition for the senior combine in Holuba Hall for pro scouts and for any other workouts I would be invited to attend. Hearing my legendary coach say I could play in the NFL fired me up.

From the 1960s through the early 2000s, countless young football players dreamed of hearing those words. To have one of the most respected coaches in the game—a man who had sent players to the College Football Hall of Fame and the NFL Hall of Fame—suggested that you could play at that level carried real weight. It was impossible not to feel validated by that belief.

Of the approximately fifteen hundred young men he coached during his head coaching career at Penn State, how many of them (who were not bona fide stars) did he really think would make decent professional football players? And then, of course, the thought has often crossed my mind: did Joe Paterno *really* believe I was capable of a solid career in the National Football League? Or had he said that to convey the rest of what he had to say?

Joe's mind was as formidable as his reputation. He understood people. As an English major and lifelong reader, Joe was familiar with the intricacies of how authors, especially our most profound writers, wove tapestries we most often referred to as characters into stories. I often tell my students that the study of literature and film is the study of ourselves. Those who study great stories, who try to put them in some kind of literary and historical context, who try to decipher the subtle as well as the grand themes within, are more apt to have a keen insight into the human condition.

Joe, a scholarly man, loved a good debate. A lot of the debates he sparked—or happily fueled—centered on where certain guys really belonged. Was Jon Witman or Curtis Enis better suited to linebacker or the offensive backfield? Was Marlon Forbes more effective at safety than at corner? Would John Sacca give us a better chance to win than Matt Nardolillo or Kerry Collins? And was Shelly Hammonds destined to be a premier tailback or a stalwart in the defensive backfield?

During an unparalleled career, Joe took part in thousands of debates and sat back wisely as his coaches went back and forth on thousands of others. I know he reveled in the process of getting the right young men in the proper positions on the field. He loved turning us loose on fall Saturdays to play out our characters, to fulfill our roles. He always said each game he coached was unique unto itself. Each told its own story. Each had its own plot lines. Win or lose, he loved the drama of it all.

Maybe the rest of his answer was an act of compassion, an understanding of the pride he knew I carried. Maybe he sensed that I would eventually hold onto the first part of what he said as one of the greatest rewards a football player could receive. Maybe there was real calculation in how he answered me. Or maybe I'm reading too much into it.

What I do know is this: the rest of his response didn't fully register until months later, after my mother had died. Only then did the words come back to me. He had paused, then said, "But if I were you, I wouldn't waste my time with pro football. You're going to be a great teacher and coach."

Long afterward, I asked myself how he had known that about me. The answer didn't come right away, but it revealed itself as I became more deeply involved in teaching and coaching. As I read my students' papers, listened to how they answered questions in class, and watched how they entered and left the room, I noticed patterns. You learn a lot if you pay attention.

A kid who couldn't sit still in class wasn't necessarily struggling with attention deficit disorder—he might have been an athlete waiting to be discovered. A sixth grader moving down the hallway with pigeon toed steps could turn out to be the school's next great sprinter. And the quiet ninth grader who took the first seat in the front row every day, arrived early, and came prepared? That student was college material, if that was the path they wanted to take.

As a coach, you learn just as much about people as does a classroom teacher. Maybe even more. The kid who is always on time for warm-ups or, if late, always comes with a note documenting a legitimate excuse from a teacher or parent. The kid who no one thought would amount to much, but s/he kept showing up to practice, kept working, kept listening to you until that one breakout performance that changed everything. The young person who was always early for practice and stayed late to help put things away but was never good enough to get in a game when it mattered. The tough-talking bully everyone feared in practice, who then spit the bit in games and would then blame everyone but himself for his/her poor play. These situations tell a lot about who you are as a human being.

Joe saw something in me that I've since seen in many of my own students. Like he may have done, I've occasionally told a small white lie—not to deceive, but to give a kid a nudge toward a future they couldn't yet imagine, even when that path seemed obvious to me.

Admitting that feels a bit like admitting you have a favorite child: some parents do, but no one says it out loud, and for good reason.

Joe wasn't a spreader of horse manure, however. As with our previous meetings, he told it the way he saw it. Either way, I appreciated the first part of his answer. When the time came, it helped me let go, with no regrets, of my professional football ambitions—no easy task for a young man who had all the tools to have a legitimate shot at an NFL career. I have to assume, given the caliber of the man, that Coach Paterno saw all this coming and accounted for it in our talk. It made an incalculable difference in my life.

Me, on the field at Beaver Stadium

An Icon Passes On

Without thinking too much about it, many of us harbor the notion that people we constantly see in the mass media will always be there. They become household names to us. They become part of the fabric, the essence of our awareness of what is important. This idea becomes fully justified when we have overtly emotional, if not physical, responses when we hear of the passing of a famous person. Often, it is not until that very moment that we realize how attached we were to that person, usually a person we've had no face-to-face relationship with at all. It brings me no shame in admitting I sobbed when the world lost Michael Jackson.

I sat alone in the dark, watching the powerful, at times gut-wrenching, memorial for him on television at the Los Angeles Lakers home arena, the Staples Center, while simultaneously posting my thoughts on Facebook with those equally interested and moved. I came of age in the seventies and eighties, the decades in which Michael's music ruled the airwaves. His music played constantly in the background of my childhood. Whether during mundane moments in the house with the family, at a house party in someone's living room or basement, during the holidays, on my Walkman (remember those?), or in complete privacy, he was there.

His persona (if not his life) and his songs projected an innocence, an unquestionable commitment to the better angels of our character, to our humanity. His undying devotion to the only race that counts, the human race, was palpable in the amazing collection of work he created and left with us. I, like so many around the world, wept tears of sorrow and thanks.

But I think we also mourned so heavily because we knew every single step we took, for the rest of our lives, would land in a world with one less mighty individual who dedicated his life to uplifting us, affirming the difficult to find notion that the impossible is indeed possible, even if only throughout a profound and catchy song. Other people had Elvis, Morrison, Lennon, Joplin, Hendrix, JFK, or MLK Jr. My generation had Michael.

I comprehend and respect the loss experienced by those who knew Joe Paterno yet never met him personally, through the prism of my admiration for Michael Jackson. Penn State football games, for some, were like Michael Jackson concerts for others. Wearing a silver glove, black leather pants with a red leather jacket, a studded belt, and a properly moist Jheri curl hairstyle and the like, was a uniform of sorts for an entire generation, similar to Penn State football fans bathing themselves, their spouses, their kids, their vehicles, and their homes in Nittany Lion blue and white. For many, my coach and mentor's glasses, rolled up slacks and black shoes, were just as iconic, if not, more so.

Joe Paterno died at 9:25 on the morning of Sunday, January 22, 2012. I knew early that day that he likely wouldn't make it. I woke, as I usually did, around six o'clock. What was different was the dream—it didn't dissolve as consciousness took over. I almost never remember my dreams. In my entire life, only three have stayed with me in vivid detail. Two were about my parents.

The third came just before my eyes opened that Sunday morning. In it, Joe and I were saying goodbye.

When I fully woke, I was shaken. I'm not someone who places unquestioned faith in dreams, astrology, or religion. I was baptized in the Anglican Church of England, went to convent school as a boy, and attended a Protestant church and Sunday school nearly every weekend of my youth, right up through my confirmation at fourteen. Even so, I've long considered myself an agnostic with strong atheistic leanings. I hold those views with conviction, though I've never felt the need to recruit anyone to them.

And yet, I've never been able to completely dismiss the mystical. My religious upbringing and Caribbean heritage won't quite allow it. So, while I don't live my life guided by dreams or their interpretations, I also couldn't brush this one aside. It lingered—quiet, unresolved—and unmistakably tied to Joe.

I turned to my wife and mentioned my dream, then went about my Sunday morning routine of watching and reading the news, hoping to hear or read that Joe had taken a positive turn. Those who are left behind rarely accept the idea of impending death regarding someone with whom we feel heavily connected. My dream prepared me for the news that came that morning.

On Facebook and via text messages, a steady volley of communications streamed between various football brothers and me beginning that morning and remaining steady for the forty-eight hours that followed. We tried to decide when we would head to State College to pay our respects to our teacher, his family, and each other.

I was picked up at my Uniondale home the following Tuesday at 5 a.m. by former teammate Vin Stewart ('94), who lived in East Meadow, the next town, less than ten minutes away if you hit all the stoplights right. On the Grand Central Parkway in New York, we met up with Gerald Filardi ('96), his wife, and three boys. During the trip up, Vin and I laughed and joked about various things we always find funny about our past or present lives. We made it to State College in under four hours. The time flew.

The line stretched outside in central Pennsylvania in January—cold, damp, unrelenting. Grown men stood shoulder to shoulder, former classmates and players Joe had coached across six decades, all quietly reconnecting. The air carried an undercurrent of grief that didn't need words. You could feel it in the silence; in the way no one complained about the wait.

We stood there for more than two hours, former players—brothers—all of us wanting to be near Joe one last time. When we finally reached the chapel, Jay Paterno was there waiting. I embraced him and told him, honestly, that I did not envy the impossible task he had faced—holding himself together well enough to fulfill his coaching responsibilities in the weeks after his father was fired. I told him how proud I was of the way he had carried himself, how well he had represented his family and all of us.

Jay cried immediately—hard, unguarded tears—for the ten or fifteen seconds we shared. Then he gathered himself, straightened up, and turned to greet Vinnie, Gerald, and the thousands who would follow us that day. I don't know that I'll ever fully be able to articulate how deeply impressed I am by how Jay handled the final months of his father's life. It's impossible for me to imagine Joe—or the generations that came before him—feeling anything but pride as the Penn State world embraced Jay, one person at a time.

Before leaving the chapel, I was next in line to speak briefly with Sue Paterno. For reasons I still don't fully understand, I had managed to hold myself together with Jay. I couldn't do the same as I approached Sue. While waiting, my eyes searched for something to steady me. I fixed my gaze on Joe's casket—and on Trey Bauer, former linebacker and one of my predecessors as Penn State Football Letterman's Club President, standing guard beside it. I was grateful for Trey's presence. It felt right that he was there.

As emotion rose in my throat, I shifted my attention again, this time to Jay, still standing strong as he embraced more of my teammates—my brothers. That did me in. The tears came fast, threatening to spill over. I didn't want that, so I turned my attention to Sue, patiently listening to the two women in front of me as they shared their stories. I remember wondering how many stories she listened to that day, how many lives passed before her, one after another, each carrying their own version of Joe.

Then came my turn.

Holding both of Sue's hands, tears finally falling without restraint, I told her about a moment that had stopped me cold years earlier. In the spring of 2007, I brought Andrew Quarless to campus for his first visit during a football clinic. I coached Andrew at my alma mater, Uniondale High School, as an assistant football coach under Greg Didio, who was my head coach when I played. Andrew had the main road through Uniondale named after him, Andrew Quarless Way, after he became a Super Bowl champion during his rookie season with the Green Bay Packers. Andrew had an excellent career at Penn State. While we were in Joe's office during his first trip to State College and the PSU football facilities, my eyes landed on something on his desk—something that stunned me into silence. I had never seen it there before, but I recognized it instantly.

From elementary school through tenth grade, my mother and I spent countless evenings doing needlepoint together. We made place settings and tissue box covers, which I sold to my teachers and the mothers of my friends. It was my first job. It paid surprisingly well—twenty dollars a tissue box cover—but what mattered far more was the time. We would sit side by side in the den, needle and thread moving in quiet rhythm as the television played in the background. Each piece took patience and care. I loved the work, but I loved being with her more.

I had no idea she had made one for Joe. Not then. Not during my playing days. I wouldn't learn that truth until more than a decade after I'd left Penn State—and eleven years after my mother had died.

I told Sue how hard it had been to steady myself enough to ask Joe about it. It had been years since I'd thought about tissue box covers, or needlepoint, or those quiet nights with my mother. And yet there it was, sitting on Joe's desk—nearly alone, surrounded by very little else—a blue tissue box cover I knew, without question, my mother had made.

"Joe, do you know who made that tissue box cover on your desk?" I had already prepared to hear him say no.

"Your mother," he shot back with much less hesitation than I anticipated. I was generally floored. This man coached over a thousand young men as the head football coach at Penn State, more if you add those he coached during his sixteen years as an assistant coach at PSU. He coached many men way more famous than me, many men I think he was closer to than he was to me, many other mothers and fathers who I assumed sent him various keepsakes. But he had a Gloria Anita Williams-made, mostly Penn State blue, tissue box cover on his neat desk. My mother never told me she made one for him. Why wouldn't I be staggered? Mom kept this from me when it was something we shared together. And Joe, even after having it for so long, instantly revealed it was from her. Staggered only begins to describe how I felt.

I explained to Sue how appreciative my parents had been for Joe and her taking care of their son and the rest of us. She thanked me, then told me that Joe had not been ready to go. Whatever strength I had left in me disappeared. It took me a long five minutes to compose myself before I could walk out of that chapel and into a battery of cameras and news people. I'm thankful for Gerald's oldest son's kindness, recognizing my suffering, in giving me a napkin. And for the strength of the Paterno family.

That same Tuesday evening, a private gathering of Penn State football brothers was organized. Many thanks to my brother and teammate, Keith Conlin, for organizing a grand affair. Among those with whom I got to spend quality time (besides Gerald and Vinnie) were Wally Richardson, Eric Gallman, Kerry Collins, Joe Jurevicius, Lance Libiano, and Clint Seace. All of us were undergrads during the ninties. We played together, so it was natural that we ended up together. There were many other brothers with whom I connected, forging or reacquiring bonds that will never be broken.

On Wednesday afternoon, I watched Joe's funeral procession move down College Avenue from the second floor of the Allen Street

Grill, standing beside Brett Conway, one of the great kickers in PSU history. Around us were diners who, like us, had come hoping for a clear view of the moment. It felt both deeply real and strangely surreal. Afterward, Vin and I began the long drive back to Long Island.

How will I remember Joe Paterno? I remember being in full squad meetings during my undergrad years where he, always teaching, would say, "I don't care what you think about me right now. I'll care what you think ten years after you've left." Well, for me, it's been thirty years plus. It will soon be sixty plus years for my oldest football brothers.

With the benefit of time, distance, and a careful look at everything that has happened at Penn State since I earned my degrees in 1995 and 1998, I remain a JoePa guy. That stance comes from reflection and research, not nostalgia or blind loyalty.

Everything I've written here, taken together, is how I felt about Joe. I was grateful that he honored the promise he made to my parents. Grateful that he was hard on me. Grateful that he was honest with me at every turn. Grateful that he tried to be fair, even when he knew he couldn't always be. Grateful that he demanded I become a Penn State graduate—twice. Grateful for his sense of honor, his courage, and for being so much more than an average man in an extraordinary role.

He once told me that people like me were his legacy. I came to understand how true that was. I carried that legacy freely, calmly, and with deep pride. Even now, whenever I find myself in the presence of another part of that legacy—especially one of my football brothers, no matter the era—I feel compelled to embrace them. Each of us carries a piece of him. And wherever we go, he goes with us.

In that sense, we each carry PhJs—doctorates in Joe's philosophy for living a successful life. I walk the world as a confident man in part because I belong to a rare brotherhood: men slow to commit serious wrongs, men who finish what they start, men who get up quickly when knocked down. We strive to love and respect one another, to honor our opponents, and to accept that success will come more often than failure—not always, but often enough.

We were also taught that even though sometimes by winning, you really lose, and sometimes in losing you really win, losing or winning shouldn't occupy the bulk of your attention. The disaster isn't in losing, nor does the triumph reside in victory. The aim is to enjoy, appreciate and respect the journey, especially and most profoundly, the parts where we must venture together. It's the road and *how* we negotiate our journey, that makes winning and losing significant.

Carrying that philosophy forward, we know what is expected of us. We continue to make Penn State proud. We must.

This is our way. This is who we are. This is who we will be.

We are... Penn State.

Overtime

Love and Loyalty

I love Penn State.

When we say that we love something or someone, we ought to be able to express, the best way we can, what that means. In total, this personal memoir, detailing my relationship with one of the world's top institutions of higher learning, is itself an explanation of the ongoing love affair I have with the place I called home for about six years as I earned my bachelor's and first master's degrees. If I had to paint the most specific picture possible outlining why I love Penn State, it comes down to this: Joe Paterno. He built his idea of a successful football program, founded on the still unique philosophy that in a world bent on

Holding my youngest son in Penn State swag during a PSU football weekend. Photo credit: Adeola Tella-Williams.

venerating while largely exploiting the athletic prowess of collegiate football players (they play for pay now, making them professionals, but without the safeguards afforded National Football League players, like collective bargaining, a clear tax payer status, pensions, or a universally accepted salary and medical benefits structure), he would recruit such gifted young men from varying backgrounds to an agricultural college in central Pennsylvania, demanding they challenge themselves intellectually and spiritually, not just athletically.

Coach Paterno recognized the exploitative nature of college football at the most fundamental level. As an Italian American playing football at Brown University in Providence, Rhode Island, he was targeted with derogatory terms like "dago," "guinea," or "wop." Joe recognized that it was and still is difficult to live in State College for four years with darker skin without being referred to by some slur, usually after two in the morning by a very drunk Penn State football fan. While playing football at Brown in the 1940s, Joe could relate. He made this crystal clear to other African American players and to me after what was, to us, an infamous visit to the Mormon Temple during an extended trip to play Brigham Young University during the 1992 season. That was when I began to truly understand how much Joe really saw and respected his darker-complexioned players, as well as how much we needed to see and respect him.

Everyone who cares about Joe knows his story. He attended Brooklyn Prep, a Jesuit school in the Crown Heights section of Brooklyn, New York, and was a member of the class of 1945. My mother was born in 1943; my father in 1950. You can find stories of various graduates who claim it was the most challenging school they ever attended. Coach Paterno studied Latin and Greek there while also gaining a major appreciation for sports, leading him to become a star football player at Brown University, where to this day he remains tied for most interceptions in a season as a defensive back (14) and is number one in Brown history for interception return yards (290). In his prime, Joe never reached the athletic ability of the vast majority of players he coached but, he was as smart if not smarter than most of his players and men with whom he coached.

Joe's iron will, it seems to me, was a product of years of deep commitment to a life of the mind as well as growing up being a kid who didn't look like a WASP. He viewed differently people who read widely. He respected them differently, although this didn't mean he looked down on those who didn't have the chance or desire to read as much. Waiting outside his office, you would find periodicals to read on anything except sports. I loved the message that was sent. The first time I noticed this was early February of 1993, the spring semester of my sophomore year. I waited to speak to him privately for the first time. This noticing confirmed who I already was at that moment.

In my bedroom growing up in Uniondale, New York, my mother, who was a registered nurse, was gifted by the family of one of her patients a collection of every issue of *National Geographic* magazine dating from 1956 to 1985. She then got me a subscription, which enabled me to acquire every issue from 1986 until I left for Penn State in June 1991. I also had a complete vintage set of the *Encyclopedia Britannica*, which was gifted to me by another family. Additionally, my strong will comes from having to fight a lot in my Long Island hometown from the time I arrived as a British West Indian immigrant in third grade until grade six. I wasn't a punk. Win or lose, you were going to know you were in a fight. I had a British accent that may have made me seem soft to some of the "Black," "White," Latino, and Asian kids with whom I grew up. For a while, I was regularly tested.

Many who played for Joe resonated with his intellect, even as we'd often be caught off guard or stupefied by it. The fire that burned hot within him came from a challenging, supportive home environment, a love of competition, and haters who enjoyed overtly underestimating, if not mocking, a skinny wop from Brooklyn who didn't belong anywhere near the Gilded Age wealth of Providence, Rhode Island. A high percentage of men who played for Joe had a similar fire and a large chip on their shoulders. This was an essential ingredient of his "Grand Experiment." Regardless of geographic location, ethnicity, or complexion, Joe recruited into his fold a very high percentage of young men who resembled him.

So, I love Penn State because I love the man who, more than anyone else, made the university what it had become at the time of his death, while leaving behind a foundation, a culture, that remains intact, despite the best efforts of many who tried to bury it. How do I know Joe's culture remains? Because people like me continue to live, breathe, and behave in a manner that honors who he was and what he stood for. Joe continues to live in me. True death occurs when no one feels any need to mention your name. We live on either because we did enormous good or committed vast savagery.

Epilogue

During the fall 1995 season, we didn't have captains. Joe had so much respect for the class of 1991. We were considered by some sports sources of the time the number one class in America coming out of high school. We continue to be considered one of, if not the very best, football classes in Penn State football history. My class was seminal to the 1994 undefeated season. Four of the five linemen anchoring that team were from my class, two of them also from Long Island, Andre Johnson and Marco Rivera. It was a monstrously talented class.

By our redshirt senior year, Coach Paterno was not comfortable naming only four or five of us captains for the season. So, he decided to name game captains for each game that season. He named offensive, defensive, and special-teams captains for each game.

Penn State football letterman wall replica in my home.

By this time in my career, I had practiced very well as a backup to the outstanding Fred Scott while also contributing to all our special teams. As a reward for not totally giving up once I lost my starting blue jersey during the 1993 season, Joe named me the special teams captain twice. I assume a couple of others received this honor, but I'm certain most did not. I was perceived as a leader by our head coach and the players. I was outspoken in the locker room during practices, during halftimes, and on the sidelines. I made sure to sit with different teammates during breakfast, lunch, and dinner, as Joe had us do during the 1993 season. I wanted to make sure younger teammates learned how to carry themselves once they became upperclassmen.

So, I suppose it's no accident that as I write this sentence, I am in the midst of my second year serving as president of the Penn State Football Letterman's Club. I'm extremely honored to hold this position. Our club is unique. Founded in 1980 by Tom Donchez and Dr. Ray "Buddy" Tesner, it is a social club focused on keeping our approximately 2,000 members connected to one another and to the football program for which we sweat and bled. The position affords me the opportunity to interact with an abundance of Penn Staters—trustee members, administrators, professors, coaches, and especially lettermen, whether they graduated in the 1950s or last year. I absolutely love it.

PSU football letterman and vice president of the PSFLC, Dr. Omar Easy, and I at a golf outing representing our almost 2,000 members.

A few things make our club exceptionally unique. First, Penn State University has, for many years now, granted us a dedicated lounge in Beaver Stadium exclusively for our select guests and us. Second, going back at least to the 1990s, lettermen have access to sideline passes for all home games until the day we die. Finally, the chief reason our club continues to thrive is that about 1,500 of our members played for one head coach. The graduating football classes from 1967 through 2013 had this one monumentally significant head football coach in common. We are bound together by our stories of him visiting our homes, cussing at us with his favorite cuss phrase ("Aw, that's horse manure!"), screaming at us to get off the ground, or telling us how much he loves us at our senior banquets. There's so much more I could go into, but most of it is for us alone.

PSU football lettermen Steve Davis ('73) and Dr. Justin S. Williams ('95/'98)

However, I am not the president of the Joe Paterno Football Letterman's Club. We have almost fifteen years' worth of players, about 500, who had a different football head coach at Penn State. Most of these men have played for James Franklin. One of my main priorities for the rest of my tenure is to build more bridges between these eras within our club. This will continue to happen in part because Coach Franklin did a phenomenal job of paying homage to the DNA of our program while blazing his own path. He regularly mentioned the lettermen, never permitted nine different iterations of our uniform, made the upgraded facilities open to all lettermen whenever we were back in town, and continued the tradition of bringing on many program letter winners as staff. We're still linebacker U, but we've also become tight end U. We still play tough as shit defense and still punish you with our running game. And? The players he recruited continue to remind me of the guys I played with, as well as the many football alumni I've grown close to since I left the program as an undergraduate. Penn State football teams continue to be full of well-spoken young men who respect the legacy upon which they continue to build.

My lower back hurts every day. I can still do some impressive things athletically, but the pain after is inevitable now. When I was young, no one on the Penn State football team or track team could beat me in a short sprint. It was the prime of life.

I got to study greatness, true greatness, in the visages of my teammates and our head coach. Sometimes, I'd be the last out of the locker room after a practice, surrounded by the beautiful mess, evidence of extraordinary feats of athleticism that would flabbergast the casual onlooker, routine for us—white athletic tape, balled up or stringy, laying haphazardly; varied shapes of dirt, recently fallen from beneath cleats trained to ferociously claw away at grassy fields as we focused on highly disciplined movements with stunning Mount Nittany, gleaming, eternal, in the early morning or late afternoon backdrop; the raw, pungent air, a not so inviting amalgam of sod, flesh and sweat, along with blood, all the cost of getting a little bit better each day.

Even in the midst of the ups and downs, I breathed in and noticed as much as possible. The great ones probably didn't have the time to deeply internalize how extraordinary our experiences were. They likely couldn't afford the time to write down any of what they saw, heard, or felt. They didn't think to document the significant stories from all their big moments—there were just too many. I don't think greatness has the luxury of regular reflection. Greatness exists to be admired and appreciated from without. It's too brilliant, powerful, and fleeting to be carefully observed from within. This is why the greatest players rarely become the greatest coaches, regardless of the sport.

The greatness of Penn State football under the guidance of Joe Paterno was that regardless of our backgrounds or complexions, he required us to be erudite, wise and tenacious; to learn how to see each other; to gain Penn State degrees; to never lay on the ground longer than necessary; to respect the man in front of you trying to defeat you; to be the best possible version of yourself while maintaining good habits and ethics; to never compromise who you are for the sake of a few wins.

Joe Paterno was teaching us how to be what he was, what our

families wished for us to be when our time with him was up. He cared for us. He protected us. In exchange for fulfilling his many requirements, our immense effort and talents made him famous, building one of the most recognizable brands in the world.

Joe Paterno with Dr. Justin S. Williams, twelve years post-graduation

In life, we must have a code. Once acquired, follow it. Do not compromise your code for any reason. There will be moments when this is hard for you. Those will be the moments where it is even more important to live your creed. Whether you fail or conquer, outcomes are fleeting, given the right mindset. Outcomes are less important than the rest of it—the journey. Do things the right way, find people you trust and can love, figure out how to journey with them. You'll go further together than you will alone, even if you can't go as quickly.

How we live is more important than how we die.

Thank you for this final lesson, Joe, my Àgbà.

References

Penn State versus University of Miami, October 12, 1991:https://www.deseret.com/1991/10/12/18945624/penn-state-vs-miami-highlights-grid-action/.

GoPSUSports, November 2, 2011: https://gopsusports.com/news/2011/11/02/penn-state-football-tied-for-best-graduation-success-rate-among-bcsap-top-25-teams.

Penn State versus University of Miami, October 10, 1992: https://youtu.be/OXiUpVkj2eQ?si=91leup4ZloSoMtZ2&t=720

Penn State versus West Virginia University, October 24, 1992: https://youtu.be/Wxhqcp6fFQc?si=aJoL-D-Pz7CV5F2O&t=4182 and https://youtu.be/Wxhqcp6fFQc?si=AqAsoYiTp9pAvAvR&t=4740

Joe Paterno is in Brown University's Sports Hall of Fame and is a member of Brown's 125th anniversary team: https://brownbears.com/sports/2018/5/8/browns-125th-anniversary-team-football.

Appendix A

No matter how you feel about Joe Paterno—or about Penn State football—there is no honest way to tell a Penn State story without acknowledging the Jerry Sandusky scandal and the lasting damage it caused. The human cost is central to it. Children were harmed. Families were shattered. Trust was broken. And the ripples have touched every corner of the university community, including those of us who wore the uniform with pride and later watched the name "Penn State" become shorthand for something we never imagined it would represent.

This book is not a legal brief, and it is not an attempt to relitigate a tragedy. It is, however, an account of the Joe I knew—formed through proximity, experience, and time. Because the scandal has so thoroughly altered how people interpret everything connected to Joe and the program, I'm including this appendix to point readers toward a deeper examination of the events, the reporting, the decisions, and the competing narratives that have surrounded them.

For the most comprehensive, long-form examination I have encountered, I refer readers to the podcast *With the Benefit of Hind-*

sight, by journalists John Ziegler and Liz Habib. You can find it on whichever platform you normally listen to podcasts.

Whether you agree with its conclusions or not, it is expansive in scope and detailed in its sourcing—an attempt to walk through the full chronology rather than the most convenient version of it. If you want to understand how this tragedy was reported, investigated, debated, and absorbed into the public imagination—and how those forces reshaped Penn State's history, culture, and legacy—this is a place to begin.

Joe and Sue Paterno with Mike McQueary

The pertinent listening occurs between episode one, dated April 15, 2021, and episode 21, dated July 18, 2025. The time between 2012, when I first began writing the manuscript for this memoir, and the date of episode one of Mr. Ziegler's podcast, was a time of absolute suffering for me and anyone else who feels about Joe and Penn State the way I do. I felt obligated to review the findings of all the key sources. This means I have also listened carefully to every single episode of the podcast. It is exhaustive information you will not get anywhere else. Mr. Ziegler and Ms. Habib devoted over one hundred hours of podcasting time, plus at least ten years of research put in by Mr. Ziegler, at great cost to his own career aspirations. Based on the many episode hours, both hosts believe the following:

1. Jerry Sandusky is not a pedophile.
2. Jerry Sandusky is serving time in jail for crimes he did not commit.
3. The three Penn State administrators who served jail time for misdemeanor charges (former athletic director Tim Curley, former senior vice president for finance and

business Gary Schultz, and former Penn State President Graham Spanier) are innocent men.

4. There was no cover-up at Penn State involving Joe Paterno and the three administrators named above to protect the reputation of the Penn State football program and the Penn State brand from any crimes of which Sandusky was found guilty.
5. Penn State has paid at least one hundred million dollars in settlements to men who were not victims of Jerry Sandusky because doing so was perceived by Penn State trustees to be cheaper than putting up a robust legal defense.
6. Once it was clear that Penn State was not going to defend itself against any allegation that Jerry Sandusky sexually victimized boys on Penn State's campus, made by any willing man who could prove he knew Jerry Sandusky as a child through his Penn State affiliated Second Mile organization, the real scandal became the list of individuals who economically victimized Penn State, directly or indirectly.

I have teammates and PSU football brothers who do not want anything more to do with this situation. Trials and verdicts were held, and punishments were imposed on individuals, the university, and our football program. Justice is blind, right? The tricky part about loyalty is knowing when to walk away from your carefully built allegiance.

Acknowledgments

Writing a book requires one to be quite selfish, causing the always veiled, if not overt, angst and consternation in those around you who love you. In this regard, I have only one person to whom I must apologize, my wife, Adeola. I am so sorry, my dear! But it is because of your existence in my life that I was finally able to fulfill a desire whose roots go back to the time to which this work is so dedicated. Thank you for bringing into my life the calm and peacefulness I needed to finally write and write and write.

Dad, my athletic life began in London, England, watching your star shine as a fast bowler for the Dulwich Croquet and Cricket Club in the 1970s. You were a much more impressive physical specimen in your prime than I was. At six foot four inches tall and 220 pounds, you were an imposing presence opposite the most skilled batsman who ever had to face you, a fast bowler. But you were extremely handy at bat as well.

Dennis Anthony and Gloria Williams

I fondly recollect being treated like a celebrity around the athletic grounds of the club, as well as inside the locker room before and after matches. It was made clear to me, both directly and indirectly, that it was a bit of a big deal being the son of Dennis Anthony Williams. This, as for so many excellent athletes with a pedigree, was how I began to learn to expect great things of myself, not only in the athletic arena, but also in the game of life.

You rarely missed any game in any sport I would later play when we relocated to Uniondale, New York. You attended my sporting events so often that I wouldn't feel completely ready to play until I could find you in the stands. There isn't an athlete I grew up with who can say their father attended more athletic functions than you did. Many times, you were the dad driving other men's sons to and from games.

Mothers get talked about all the time. And deservedly so. Too often, fathers like you get lost in the shuffle of the affections showered on mommies. For reasons known to both you and me, Dad, I'll not have this moment pass without giving you your proper due. Life had to give me a pretty good beating before I could fully realize this fact: You, more than any other ingredient in my life, have been the decisive cause of any success I have attained. No matter what I do, no matter where I may travel, I continue to see you in the stands looking out at me. I'm still trying to play well for you, Dad.

Much love and appreciation are due to the first football coaches I ever had, assistant coach Dave Wibben and head coach Al Blau. During that year, I was in the eighth grade, Coach Blau was full of energy, passion, and was able to teach and motivate without cursing or ever speaking loudly in anger, although he screamed his head off! Coach Blau taught me the basics of the game and saw my potential. A local star was born under your loving tutelage. The impact of your great, great soul will always be felt. Coach Wibben attended every game I coached as a varsity head coach, many years after coaching me as a defensive back during my first two years playing football. He never cussed and was grounded by his strong Christian faith. Rest in power, Coach.

My varsity football coaches continued what my junior high

school coaches started. Huge love and appreciation to assistant coaches Greg Johnson, Ray O'Keefe, and Phil Coppola, as well as head coach Greg Didio. The effort and dedication of these men poured into my teammates and me will never be forgotten. It is because of them, as well as my great teammates, that I was able to display enough talent on the football field to be identified as something special by so many universities. I will always be thankful that Coach Didio met with me in the mornings, an hour and a half before school began, spring semester of my sophomore year, to throw the football around in the boys' gym of Uniondale High School. He taught me how to be a quarterback, a leader, reinforcing the significance of going the extra mile and learning why it's never crowded. Coach O'Keefe was a grizzled lover of sports with a tough, raspy voice to match. He made his players on defense want to be tough for him. We loved playing for him.

Very special love and appreciation go to Greg Johnson and Phil Coppola. They didn't just coach me in high school. They became my friends. I eventually had the privilege of coaching alongside them and head coach Anthony Mascia at Holy Trinity High School in Hicksville, Long Island, my first coaching experience.

The very first time I set foot on the amazing University Park campus at Penn State, Phil drove me. He and Greg laid the blueprint for the sort of relationship I wished to have with players I would eventually coach. In some cases, I think I achieved it. I have a great deal of respect and admiration for you both.

Phil, you treated me like your little brother. I was with you during some of my happiest times and when I received the worst news of my life. We shared great joys and massive sorrows. You were an enormous light in my life from the time I was seventeen and for a decade after. I thank you for making me a comfortable part of your circle during that time in our lives. I cannot overstate your impact on me as a young man. I will love you forever.

I must also thank Michael Ninivaggi and Tricia, the mother of his children, for their support during my undergraduate years. You guys also treated me like family. The dinners at Damon's after games in State College and your constantly positive words sustained me through difficult times. Many thanks to you both.

I want to also recognize the men and women everywhere who managed to play competitive sports in college but didn't have things turn out the way they wished—the vast majority of college athletes in the country. Also, all those men and women who wanted badly to play competitive sports in college for a team and/or coach they admired or loved but couldn't. Hopefully, each of you will find a story you can respect, embedded within the fabric of my account.

Mom and Dad, thank you for raising me the way you did. Thank you for loving me the way parents should love their children. With every single step and exhalation, I live to honor your names.

About the Author

Justin Williams has been an English teacher for four decades, shaping students' and student-athletes' understanding of social justice, identity, and self-empowerment. A New York State certified English teacher and school administrator, he often tells his students, "*The study of literature and film is the study of ourselves.*" Throughout his career, he has taught English in grades 6–12 in both the United States and the United Arab Emirates and has also taught at the collegiate level at Penn State University and Hofstra University.

A full-scholarship football player at Penn State, Justin was a three-year letterman while earning his bachelor's degree in English education and a minor in African American Studies ('95). He went on to complete a master's degree in education administration ('98) at Penn State, followed by a certificate of advanced studies ('18) and a doctorate in education leadership and policy studies, with an emphasis on career and technical education, from Hofstra University ('23).

The son of Jamaican and Trinidadian parents, Justin is a "third culture kid" who grew up in London, England, before moving to Uniondale, New York. He is a lifetime member of both the Penn State Alumni Association and the Penn State Football Lettermen's

Club (PSFLC), serving as president of the latter since the spring of 2024. He has also served on the executive board of the Sigma Beta Beta Chapter (Nassau County, New York) as a proud member of the Omega Psi Phi Fraternity, Inc.

bsky.app/profile/drjwilliams27.bsky.social

About the Publisher

Highlander Press is more than a publishing house—we're a movement.

Founded in 2019, Highlander Press exists to elevate powerful stories that inspire change, spark conversation, and expand what's possible. We specialize in guiding purpose-driven authors—from initial concept to beautifully published book—with clarity, confidence, and unparalleled support.

Our model is intentionally collaborative. We work hand in hand with each author to demystify the publishing process, champion creative integrity, and deliver top-tier results without the smoke and mirrors. Every author who walks through our doors is seen, heard, and supported—because we know that behind every great book is a courageous voice ready to rise.

At Highlander Press, you're not just publishing a book—you're stepping into your next chapter as a leader, a visionary, and a changemaker.

instagram.com/highlanderpress
facebook.com/highlanderpress
tiktok.com/highlanderpress
linkedin.com/company/highlander-press

www.ingramcontent.com/pod-product-compliance
Lightning Source LLC
Chambersburg PA
CBHW040051180826
50016CB00043B/821
* 9 7 8 1 9 5 6 4 4 2 6 9 4 *